HE WORLD MONETARY SYSTEM

*A Statement on National Policy
by the Research and Policy Committee
of the Committee for Economic Development
July 1973*

Single copy . . . $1.50

Printed in U.S.A.
First Printing July 1973
Design: Harry Carter
Library of Congress Catalog Card Number: 73-84800
International Standard Book Number: 0-87186-051-1

Committee for Economic Development
477 Madison Avenue, New York, N. Y. 10022

Contents

The Responsibility
for CED Statements on National Policy

This statement has been approved for publication as a statement of the Research and Policy Committee by the members of that Committee and its drafting subcommittee, subject to individual dissents or reservations noted herein. *The trustees who are responsible for this statement are listed on pages 5 and 6. Company associations are included for identification only; the companies do not share in the responsibility borne by the individuals.*

The Research and Policy Committee is directed by CED's bylaws to:

"Initiate studies into the principles of business policy and of public policy which will foster the full contribution by industry and commerce to the attainment and maintenance of high and secure standards of living for people in all walks of life through maximum employment and high productivity in the domestic economy."

The bylaws emphasize that:

"All research is to be thoroughly objective in character, and the approach in each instance is to be from the standpoint of the general welfare and not from that of any special political or economic group."

The Research and Policy Committee is composed of 60 Trustees from among the 200 businessmen and educators who comprise the Committee for Economic Development. It is aided by a Research Advisory Board of leading economists, a small permanent Research Staff, and by advisors chosen for their competence in the field being considered.

Each Statement on National Policy is preceded by discussions, meetings, and exchanges of memoranda, often stretching over many months. The research is undertaken by a subcommittee, with its advisors, and the full Research and Policy Committee participates in the drafting of findings and recommendations.

Except for the members of the Research and Policy Committee and the responsible subcommittee, the recommendations presented herein are not necessarily endorsed by other Trustees or by the advisors, contributors, staff members, or others associated with CED.

The Research and Policy Committee offers these Statements on National Policy as an aid to clearer understanding of the steps to be taken in achieving sustained growth of the American economy. The Committee is not attempting to pass on any pending specific legislative proposals; its purpose is to urge careful consideration of the objectives set forth in the statement and of the best means of accomplishing those objectives.

Research and Policy Committee

1. Voted to approve the policy statement but submitted memoranda of comment, reservation, or dissent, or wished to be associated with memoranda of others. See pages 83 to 87.

6.

Foreword

The devaluation of the U.S. dollar late in 1971 and again in February 1973 led first to numerous foreign exchange crises and then to the floating of all the major noncommunist currencies. By now it is obvious that monetary reform has become essential to restore some measure of order to the world international financial system.

The impact of substantial dollar devaluation during the past two years clearly led to floating of the major noncommunist currencies. This condition has brought increasing recognition of the urgent need to make progress toward new international monetary rules to replace the Bretton Woods system, a subject that undoubtedly will be on the agenda of the meeting of the International Monetary Fund in September.

This statement deals in some detail with the events which have led to the monetary crisis and with reforms that are essential to resolve it. It also describes essential changes that should be made, without attempting to suggest the finite details of a new monetary system. However, it does stress that despite the weakness of the dollar in foreign exchange markets the United States must "exert strong leadership" in any forthcoming reform of the international monetary system. The point is also made that the United States already has taken some constructive initiatives in this direction.

It is the view of this Committee that a reformed monetary system must not only foster a more efficient allocation of world resources but also permit individual member countries enough leeway to accomplish their domestic economic objectives. At the same time the Committee regards it as essential to eliminate the extremely large payments imbalances that now exist if the monetary system is to function in a reasonably smooth manner.

To achieve these goals, it urges that two basic conditions be met: first, that the United States pursue domestic economic policies that ensure high employment without demand or cost inflation while at the same time strengthening its productivity and competitiveness; and, second, that the structure of the international monetary system shift both its rules and organization to the extent necessary to handle problems that have beset it in the past and those which may challenge it in the foreseeable future.

On behalf of the Research and Policy Committee I express our appreciation to all members of the Subcommittee on Reform of the International Monetary System which prepared the statement. I should particularly like to acknowledge the superb leadership of its chairman, Howard C. Petersen, and to commend the project director, Frank W. Schiff, CED's Chief Economist, who deserves special recognition for his excellent contributions to the background research and for his competent direction of the work.

Philip M. Klutznick, *Chairman*
Research and Policy Committee

Chapter One

Introduction and Summary of Recommendations

In the past two years, the international monetary system has undergone an extraordinary succession of transformations. Formal convertibility of the dollar into gold and other reserve assets was ended in mid-1971. Since then the dollar itself has been devalued twice, and sizable adjustments have been made in the parities of other major currencies. Massive movements of funds have triggered a series of foreign exchange crises that forced the closing of international money markets for as much as several weeks at a time. By the spring of 1973, these developments had led to the floating of the currencies of all the Free World's major industrial nations.

The swift course of recent events no longer leaves any doubt about whether the world's monetary system will be reformed. A major process of change is already under way. What remains at issue is the direction that the changes will take. Will they be based on a patchwork of crisis-generated reactions to emerging events, culminating in increasingly destructive rivalries and a growing fragmentation of the international economic and financial system? Or will reform be based on positive and truly cooperative efforts to adapt the world's monetary system to the needs of today and of the coming decades?

In many respects, the recent changes in the world's monetary relationships represent important progress. The realignments of the currency parities of the major trading countries constituted long-overdue steps to correct the very large imbalances in their payments positions. These readjustments are likely to produce a more viable longer-run payments situation, although no one set of parities can be regarded as suitable for an indefinite period. The very fact that the adjustments were worked out in direct confrontations of top financial officials of the key countries and on the basis of mutual concessions constituted an advance over various earlier episodes of exchange rate adjustments. Moreover, the prior regime of highly rigid exchange rates has now been replaced by a wide variety of adjustment techniques, including the concerted floating of major currencies, that had previously been regarded as only remote possibilities. This has made it possible to consider the design of a more permanent monetary reform in the light of a much wider range of practical experiences than would have been feasible until now.

But the recent developments have also posed profound dangers. The continued uncertainties have shaken confidence in the monetary system. That confidence is not likely to be fully restored until it becomes clearer what type of system will be erected to modify or replace the Bretton Woods structure. Cooperative arrangements have been worked out only under crisis conditions and on a piecemeal basis. Major questions remain as to whether cooperation will in fact persist or give way to a series of competitive depreciations of major currencies and an uncoordinated proliferation of national controls over trade and capital movements. In the absence of a clear indication that there is fundamental agreement on the rules of the game and a basic willingness to abide by a central authority that will enforce these rules, the danger remains very real that the world will be moving toward a system of economic warfare among increasingly separated regional trading blocs.

Thus, there is need for early progress toward a comprehensive international monetary reform. Such a reform is required both to take advantage of the opportunities that the rapid changes in international monetary relationships have created and to prevent them from deteriorating in the direction of restrictionism and economic warfare.

This policy statement indicates the broad directions that a constructive reform should take.* The statement does not attempt to present a detailed new plan, nor does it cover all the relevant questions involved in this complex area. Rather, our purpose has been to examine a number of key issues in the light of our knowledge and experience.

We believe that in any effort to reform the international monetary system, the United States must exert strong leadership. This does not mean that the form of leadership today can be the same as it was in earlier years when the United States had a dominant position in the international economic and financial system. Nor does it imply that the United States should fail to defend its legitimate self-interests in dealing with other countries. But as the nation that still has the most powerful economy in the world, our interests basically coincide with an expanding and relatively free international economic order that will benefit all countries. Thus, there is every reason for the United States to take the lead in cooperative efforts with other major nations to build a more viable and stable world monetary system.

In this context, we commend the constructive initiatives toward designing an improved international monetary system that the U.S. government has undertaken during the past year, starting with Treasury Secretary Shultz's speech to the 1972 annual meetings of the International Monetary Fund (IMF). Our proposals build upon the basic thrust of these policy initiatives.

Basic Tasks of the International Monetary System

The functioning of the international monetary system is much like the health of the human body. When the system is working properly, its existence is taken for granted. It is only when the system works badly or begins to break down that people become aware of its importance and of the many complex ways in which it affects their lives.

Recent international monetary developments have given the ordinary citizen ample opportunities for observing why the monetary system matters. For example, the U.S. devaluation in connection with the

---

*See Memorandum by MR. THEODORE O. YNTEMA, page 83.

Smithsonian Agreement of December 1971 and the subsequent devaluation of February 1973 in combination reduced the international value of the dollar by an average of about 17 per cent in relation to all major foreign currencies. By early June 1973, moreover, the market value of the dollar vis-à-vis the pre-Smithsonian par values for the German mark and the Japanese yen had declined by about 28 per cent and 26 per cent, respectively. These developments have raised the cost of many foreign products and services for American citizens, in effect lowering their living standards. Moreover, by making purchases of U.S. goods more attractive to many foreigners, it has added substantially to foreign demand for U.S. output, thus placing pressure on already tight U.S. supplies and contributing significantly to the sharp rise in domestic prices. Indeed, housewives concerned about higher meat prices and businessmen worried about a lumber shortage must blame these problems, at least in part, on the effects of the devaluations. The exchange rate realignments, it should be stressed, were appropriate under the circumstances; but they need not have involved such large changes within a short time if the required adjustment actions had not been delayed for so many years.

The malfunctioning of the monetary system during recent years has also served to highlight some of the system's effects on jobs and business operations. Thus, the overvaluation of the dollar prior to the recent exchange rate realignments (which kept foreign prices low when translated into U.S. dollars) led to very sharp increases in imports for such products as steel and textiles. The threat of job losses for workers in U.S. industries that produce these and other items has generated major demands for protectionist measures. Moreover, adequate forward planning and future cost calculations by business have at times been hampered by uncertainties regarding the future international value of currencies and by fears that governments might impose various new restrictions on international transactions for balance-of-payments reasons.

The developments just described help to underline the basic tasks that should be performed by a well-functioning world monetary system. Such a system should:

1. Foster a more efficient allocation of world resources—and thus a general rise in living standards—by facilitating vigorous growth of multilateral trade and investment, with a minimum of restrictions;

2. At the same time, allow individual countries adequate scope to achieve their legitimate domestic economic objectives, including high employment with price stability;

3. Be sufficiently stable and crisis-free to produce general confidence in the monetary system and the principal currencies, enabling individuals and businesses to make rational plans for the future;

4. Be flexible enough to cope effectively with major or unforeseen changes in the world economy;

5. Serve to foster international political cooperation rather than become an independent source of economic and political frictions.

To achieve these goals, the international monetary system must be able to carry out three specific functions. It must provide for sufficiently prompt and effective *adjustment* of payments imbalances among individual countries; promote adequate growth in total international monetary reserves and *liquidity;* and deter excessively volatile shifts among reserve assets or individual currencies that serve to undermine *confidence* in the workings of the system as a whole.

The most difficult of these tasks has been to achieve proper payments adjustment. At the core of the difficulty is the fact that adjustment must seek to reconcile the inherent conflict between greatly increased economic and financial interdependence among nations and their simultaneous desire for strengthened autonomy to pursue national economic goals. How these conflicts are resolved depends a great deal on the choice among the principal alternative methods of adjustment that are available: (1) domestic fiscal and monetary policies that change total spending and demand; (2) exchange rate changes that directly affect relative international prices and costs; and (3) controls and related measures that impinge on particular types of international transactions, such as trade and capital movements.

The problem is that no one method will serve all of a country's goals simultaneously. Sole reliance on demand policies to eliminate a deficit, for example, may interfere with attainment of high employment. Controls interfere with freedom of international transactions. Full reliance on exchange rate changes may reduce the scope for international integration and entail greater risks on the side of inflation. Within countries, too, the choice of adjustment methods requires a difficult balancing among the interests of different groups and sectors: consumers versus producers, exporters versus importers, industry versus industry.

Later in this chapter, we shall summarize our own recommendations on how the international monetary system can best resolve these difficulties and carry out the essential tasks we have outlined. Before turning to these proposals, it is useful to examine some of the major problems that the system has faced in the past as well as the key challenges that are likely to confront it in the decades ahead.

The Bretton Woods System: Achievements and Deficiencies

When the Bretton Woods system was created in 1944, its primary task was to prevent a return to the chaotic world monetary conditions of the 1930s. The breakdown of international monetary arrangements was one of the major causes of the Great Depression during these years. In turn, it was significantly affected by that depression. One country after another had sought to restore domestic employment and output by pushing its unemployment problem on other nations. This was done through the uncoordinated use of such measures as increased import barriers, competitive exchange rate depreciations, and exchange controls. Confidence in currencies had thereby been destroyed and the volume of trade and other international transactions had shrunk disastrously.

The Bretton Woods agreement sought to restore stability and confidence in the monetary system by replacing economic warfare with rules and machinery for international cooperation. Such rules would allow countries to achieve their domestic objectives and at the same time foster sound expansion of world trade. The agreement provided for establishment of fixed exchange parities that member countries of the newly established International Monetary Fund were obligated to defend. These parities could be altered with the permission of the Fund, but only when a country's payments balance was in "fundamental" disequilibrium. Less serious imbalances were to be dealt with by temporary financing based partly on newly created IMF lending facilities, as well as through reliance on appropriate national economic policies. The system called for abolition of exchange controls over current transactions and reduction of trade barriers. It also aimed at the gradual restoration of full convertibility among currencies. Confidence in the system and provision of adequate liquidity essentially rested on the predominant role of the United States and the emergence of the dollar as the main reserve currency, although this was not a formal part of the agreement.

Until the late 1950s, the Bretton Woods arrangement worked remarkably well. World industrial output grew by about 5½ per cent a year from 1948 to 1960, and levels of employment were far higher and much more stable than in the prewar period. Moreover, world trade rose by about 7 per cent a year from 1948 to 1960, and other types of international transactions also showed a remarkable expansion. At the same time, there were unprecedented net reductions in tariff barriers and in quantitative restrictions on trade. By the late 1950s, currency convertibility among the major countries had been restored, leading to an extraordinary expansion in international capital flows.

At the very time these successes were achieved, however, the system began to run into difficulties. Payments imbalances among the major countries became very large. The United States accumulated growing deficits while continental European countries (and later Japan) registered excessive surpluses. The adjustment mechanisms available under the Bretton Woods arrangements were not adequately used to force a reduction of these huge imbalances, mainly because the system did not provide strong enough incentives for sufficiently timely and sizable changes in exchange rates. Moreover, the asymmetrical character of the arrangements that had emerged in conjunction with the Bretton Woods system now proved to be a major drawback. With the dollar serving as the main reserve currency, total international liquidity in general could only be expanded through more U.S. deficits; but as these deficits accumulated, confidence in the dollar started to erode.

In turn, the efforts that were subsequently made to restore payments equilibrium without frequent exchange rate adjustments caused a reappearance of many of the problems that the Bretton Woods system had been designed to correct. Balance-of-payments problems led to policies that excessively curtailed domestic output and employment in various countries. They also gave rise to renewed increases in restrictions on trade, aid, and capital movements. As a result, means and ends often became badly confused. The very goals that a soundly functioning payments system is supposed to achieve, such as high employment and relatively free international transactions, were all too frequently sacrificed in an effort to foster a better payments balance.

Table 1: U.S. Balance of Payments by Area, 1965 and 1972 (in billions of dollars)

	Global[a]		Western Europe		Japan		Canada		Developing Countries	
	1965	1972	1965	1972	1965	1972	1965	1972	1965	1972
Trade Balance	4.9	—6.8	2.7	—0.6	—0.4	—4.1	0.6	—1.8	1.3	—0.9
Exports	26.4	48.8	8.9	15.0	2.1	5.0	5.4	12.6	8.4	13.9
Imports	—21.5	—55.7	—6.2	—15.6	—2.4	—9.1	—4.8	—14.5	—7.2	—14.8
Current Account Balance	4.3	—8.0	1.2	—4.5	—0.4	—4.8	1.4	—0.4	1.5	0.8
Total Long-Term Capital (net)	—6.1	—1.2	—1.3	3.4	—0.1	0.3	—1.4	—1.1	—2.8	—3.3
Private Long-term Capital	—4.6	0.1	—1.2	3.5	—0.1	0.3	—1.4	—1.1	—1.3	—2.2
Basic Balance	—1.8	—9.2	—0.1	—1.1	—0.5	—4.5	0	—1.5	—1.3	—2.4
Official Settlements Balance	—1.3	—10.3	—	—	—	—	—	—	—	—

a The global figures cover more regions than are shown in the table.

Source: U.S. Department of Commerce, Survey of Current Business.

Together with the emerging weaknesses of the reserve and liquidity system, these deficiencies in the adjustment process led to increasingly frequent and serious currency crises. In contrast with the situation in the 1930s, total world output and trade continued to advance strongly even in the face of these difficulties. But the growing uncertainties resulted in more and more interferences with the pursuit of sound national economic policies as well as with orderly business planning and operations. By August 1971, the size of payments imbalances and of speculative attacks on the dollar had become large enough to result in the suspension of official dollar convertibility.

How can these developments be explained? Among the main elements of the explanation are the following:

1. The very successes of the Bretton Woods system proved to be a major source of its later difficulties. The system was one of the elements that permitted and encouraged the rapid postwar growth in the economic and financial power of European countries and of Japan. It thus also contributed to the concomitant loss by the United States of its position of overwhelming predominance in international economic affairs. An indication of the size of the recent shifts in the U.S. trade and payments relationships with Europe, Japan, and other major areas is provided by Table 1. Most striking is the fact that the overall U.S. trade position shifted from a surplus of $4.9 billion in 1965 to a deficit of $6.8 billion in 1972 (chart, page 18). In turn, the major structural changes that lay behind these shifts called for far more frequent and extensive changes in adjustment policies—and particularly in exchange rates—than the system seemed able to bring about.

2. Restoration of currency convertibility was followed by a far greater increase in the volume and volatility of capital transactions than had been envisaged when the Bretton Woods system was first created. International capital markets witnessed a wide variety of basic structural changes, including the emergence of the Eurocurrency market. These developments, in turn, created additional problems for international monetary management that existing mechanisms could not readily handle.

3. The underlying asymmetries in the system proved increasingly troublesome. In particular, the dollar's role as a reserve currency meant that the United States, unlike other countries, had relatively little scope for changing its exchange parity in order to reduce its deficits; at the

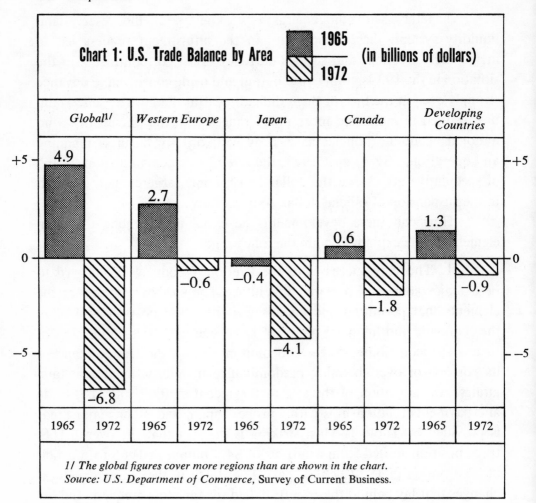

Chart 1: U.S. Trade Balance by Area — 1965/1972 (in billions of dollars)

1/ The global figures cover more regions than are shown in the chart.
Source: U.S. Department of Commerce, Survey of Current Business.

same time, the major surplus countries were generally reluctant or un-willing to revalue their currencies or take other measures to reduce their surpluses.

4. Eventual breakdown of the system was greatly hastened by severe failures of individual countries to pursue sound domestic economic policies and by the absence of sufficient political will to make use of the adjustment instruments that were available under the Bretton Woods arrangements. Clearly, the highly inflationary demand policies pursued by the United States in the latter part of the 1960s and the mounting cost-push inflation in the early 1970s were of key importance in this context. But the stubborn failures of the principal surplus countries to adopt appropriate corrective measures also played a major role.

Challenges for the Future

A first step toward the restoration of a smoothly functioning world monetary system must be the elimination of the huge existing payments imbalances that represent a legacy of the system's past malfunctioning. As already noted, the major exchange rate realignments of the past two years provide an appropriate basis for correcting the imbalances. But these measures require considerable time to take hold, and their success is by no means assured. They can only succeed if governments follow policies that will allow them to work.

Correction of existing imbalances, of course, will not by itself overcome the underlying shortcomings of the system that caused these imbalances in the first place. More basic changes in the system are required to deal with this problem. One major forward step was taken in 1968, when Special Drawing Rights (SDRs) were created to provide a more rational means of new international liquidity creation. Since 1971, moreover, a number of other important improvements have in effect already evolved, including the willingness of governments to allow greater exchange rate flexibility in particular circumstances. But the arrangements that now exist do not yet form a solid basis for fully adequate functioning of the monetary system.

The needed reforms in the monetary system must do more than cope with the problems that have affected the system in the past. They must also allow it to deal effectively with the major changes in international political, economic, and payments relationships that are likely to emerge in the coming decades. These include the continuing tendency toward greater international economic interdependence; the growing role of more closely integrated regional areas, notably the European Community; and the increasing importance of multinational corporations in international trading and investment activities. They are also likely to involve major changes in economic relationships between the United States, the European Community, and Japan; between the developed countries and the less developed nations; and between the "market" and the non-market economies.

Perhaps the most serious emerging problem stems from the possibility of major worldwide or regional shortages of various raw materials and the impact of such developments on the payments positions of industrial countries. The most dramatic changes in this area are occurring in the field of energy, particularly petroleum. It has been estimated on the basis of current trends that by 1980, the industrial countries of the Organization for Economic Cooperation and Development (OECD) may have to import more than $50 billion of oil from the "oil-producing" countries. For the United States alone, such imports could easily reach $18 to $24 billion, compared with about $4 billion in 1972. According to the President's Council on International Economic Policy, the net direct effect of oil transactions on the U.S. current account balance in 1980 could amount to an outflow of from $5 to $10 billion. Clearly, the stability of the international monetary system will be greatly influenced by the manner in which the huge earnings that the oil-producing nations are expected to accumulate will be utilized. Much will depend on whether these earnings are used for building up the economies of these countries through imports of goods and services; for investments in the industrial or less developed countries; or for maintenance of exceptionally large foreign exchange reserves that could serve as a major destabilizing factor in international capital markets. A detailed consideration of these issues lies beyond the scope of this statement; we plan to examine them in depth in a future study that will specifically focus on the world energy problem. However, their existence must be taken into full account in any efforts to design a really viable world monetary system.

SUMMARY OF RECOMMENDATIONS
Key Requirements for Effective Reform

A fundamental solution to the problems of the international monetary system will require more than agreement on particular exchange rate arrangements or on measures for coping with excessive currency speculation, although adequate resolution of these issues is clearly of major importance. In our view, no set of specific reforms can solve the underlying problems unless two basic conditions are met.

First, it is of crucial importance that the United States pursue sound domestic economic policies that will enable it to achieve high employment without excessive demand or cost inflation and that involve a significant strengthening of U.S. productivity and competitiveness. Unless such policies are adopted, the needed correction of payments imbalances made possible by the recent exchange rate realignments would be frustrated. These policies, moreover, are essential for increasing confidence in the dollar, which will continue to be the single most important currency in the international system. In particular, we consider it vitally important that

- Fiscal and monetary policies be vigorously used to prevent an excessive U.S. demand expansion;
- Major reforms in Congressional and Executive Branch budget procedures be adopted promptly so that total government spending can be brought under effective control;
- Wage-price restraints, to the extent that they can be effectively used to supplement adequate fiscal and monetary measures, be forcefully applied to help bring cost-push pressures under control;*
- Major new efforts be undertaken by government, business, labor and the farm sector to achieve a wide range of structural reforms that will make the economy more competitive and productive, along lines recommended in our July 1972 statement on *High Employment Without Inflation.*[1]

Second, the Bretton Woods structure must be recast into a set of new or substantially reformed rules and institutions that are sufficiently powerful to leave no doubt that they can effectively cope with the problems that have beset the international monetary system in past decades and that may face it in the future. This calls for a significant increase in the willingness of governments to adhere to common rules and cooperative procedures. It means, in effect, that in their mutual interest they will have to yield some added elements of sovereignty to international institutions of which they are a part. In particular, the need is for

- Effective new rules and procedures to assure sufficiently prompt adjustment of payments imbalances by both surplus and deficit countries;
- Better machinery for meaningful consultations on the compatibility of countries' balance-of-payments aims and policies;

1/*High Employment Without Inflation: A Positive Program for Economic Stabilization.* A Statement on National Policy by the Research and Policy Committee, Committee for Economic Development (New York: July 1972).
*See Memorandum by MR. JOHN D. HARPER, page 83.

● Agreement on the appropriate use of different types of policy instruments in different circumstances, especially on means of avoiding reliance on direct trade and capital controls;

● Appropriate machinery for promulgating and applying these rules, and for the use of international sanctions where necessary;

● Fully adequate means to provide for orderly growth in international liquidity and to cope convincingly with massive speculative threats to the system;

● A willingness to entrust various new operational functions to administration by an international body.

We recommend that the principal powers of international monetary management under the proposed new arrangements should be lodged in the International Monetary Fund. This calls for basic changes in the Fund's articles and administrative organization.

Assuring Adequate Adjustment

The new system should leave considerable flexibility to national governments in their choice among adjustment instruments. At the same time, new and stronger incentives must be provided to assure prompter and more effective adjustment of payments imbalances.

We favor the use of objective indicators to establish international presumption of the need for adjustment action. Such indicators should focus mainly on the results of inadequate adjustment, notably excessively large or deficient international reserve positions.[2] If a reserve test is used, we would favor emphasis on the *speed* of changes in reserves as well as on the extent of deviations from appropriate reserve levels. Use of reserve indicators would not automatically have to lead to adjustment action, since the affected countries might present valid reasons why such action

---

2/Use of presumptive indicators is especially important under par value regimes. It would, in particular, be intended to assure sufficiently frequent parity changes. A statement published as a supplement to the January 1973 Report of the President's Council of Economic Advisers presented an official U.S. proposal for using specified deviations from "base levels" of each country's international reserves as indicators of the need for balance-of-payments adjustment. Other possible presumptive indicators include the cyclically adjusted "basic" payments balance (i.e., the balance on current and long-term capital account) and the movement of spot exchange rates in relation to the permissible margins.

would not be appropriate in the particular case involved. In assessing such reasons, moreover, consideration could also be given to the behavior of various other objective indicators. However, reliance on reserve indicators would impose the burden of proof that adjustment action is not necessary on the country to which the indicators point. The proposed procedure, therefore, should significantly reduce the scope for protracted postponement of needed policy measures and help foster the more timely payments adjustments that are essential for a proper functioning of the monetary system.*

The Degree of Flexibility in Exchange Rates

Exchange rate changes must henceforth play a substantially larger role in balance-of-payments adjustment than was the case under the Bretton Woods regime. They should no longer be the adjustment instrument of last resort. Other policy instruments, to be sure, will still have to play a key role in many instances. **There should, however, be a presumption that exchange rate changes will normally be used to assist in the correction of payments imbalances, either as the instrument that is most appropriate in particular circumstances or as a second line of defense to be used promptly if other methods do not give evidence that they can achieve the needed correction within a fairly brief period of time.**

As businessmen, we are interested in having an exchange rate system that does not give rise to excessively large and unpredictable interferences with economic transactions and calculations and that relies as little as possible on the use of direct controls. Some of us have a preference for freely floating exchange rates in this connection because we believe that it will be easier for business to make rational forward plans when its main task is to anticipate the likely behavior of free markets rather than the decisions of governments. Others among us would prefer reliance on exchange rate parities subject to frequent and relatively small adjustments, on the grounds that this will in fact be more conducive to an open world economy, will be less inflationary, and will involve fewer risks of destabilizing speculation.

---

*See Memorandum by MR. FRANKLIN A. LINDSAY, page 84.

We do not consider it essential that a decision be made now on the precise future mixture between reliance on floats and on adjustable parities. The essential needs of sound international trade and finance can be met either by (a) a system of floating exchange rates involving periodic official intervention or (b) exchange parities subject to frequent and relatively small adjustments, with provisions for wider margins and options for temporary floats under appropriate circumstances.* Our own eventual preference will depend on actual experience under alternative systems. We believe that for some time to come, leeway for using a variety of approaches should remain available. In any event, we consider it inevitable that any floating exchange rate system will involve some intervention. Most governments regard the exchange rate as a highly important economic variable whose movements can have significant implications for the management of their economies; they are usually not willing to permit such rates to be completely determined by market forces. At the same time, par value systems with more frequent and smaller adjustments will have to allow for temporary floats. In terms of results, therefore, the differences between the two arrangements may not turn out to be very great. **In our view, the more important consideration is that, regardless of the exchange rate system adopted, a clear set of internationally agreed-upon rules must be developed to govern its operation.**

In most respects, the same basic types of considerations should govern the design of rules for floating rates with intervention and for par value regimes with provisions for frequent parity adjustments. In particular, rules are needed to:

- Avoid excessive interference with the amplitude and speed of exchange rate changes under floating rate regimes and encourage smaller and more frequent changes under par value systems;
- Prevent competitive devaluations that stem from attempts by individual countries to use exchange rate policy to shift their internal business-cycle problems to other countries;
- Deal with the use of direct controls and other policy instruments that countries may use in conjunction with exchange rate policy, both to affect their payments structures and to combat speculation.

---

*See Memorandum by MR. GABRIEL HAUGE, page 84.

To the extent that par values are retained, we recommend that exchange rate margins between the United States and other major countries should be somewhat wider than the margins provided under the Smithsonian Agreement. This would not prevent other countries, such as those within the European Community, from maintaining different margins in transactions with each other if they considered this appropriate. We also propose that consideration be given to the creation of an "inner band" within exchange margins in which intervention would be ruled out altogether.

The Role of Other Policy Instruments

1. *Domestic Policies*

Under any type of exchange rate system, sound domestic fiscal and monetary policies should be regarded as of fundamental importance for the maintenance of healthy international economic and monetary relationships. Such policies, however, will not eliminate the need for exchange rate changes in various situations. Under par value regimes, this is particularly true in so-called "dilemma" cases, such as the coexistence of substantial unemployment with payments deficits.

2. *Trade*

International monetary and trade negotiations should be closely coordinated so that trade liberalization and improved monetary adjustment will be able to progress in parallel.* Moreover, like the current monetary negotiations, the forthcoming trade negotiations should be conducted on a multilateral basis.

The use of trade measures for balance-of-payments adjustment should normally be limited to actions by surplus countries that *reduce* trade barriers. **Import surcharges and similar measures should not be a substitute for needed exchange rate realignments. We believe, moreover, that it would be a serious mistake for the United States or other countries to superimpose import surcharges, extensive quantitative trade restrictions, or export subsidies on top of such exchange rate changes as a means of dealing with overall payments adjustment.**

It may, however, be appropriate to authorize uniform import surcharges as an ultimate sanction against a country or countries that fail

---

*See Memorandum by MR. ROBERT O. ANDERSON, page 85.

to take proper exchange rate or other action to curb excessive payments surpluses. The U.S. government should have legislative authority to make use of such measures. But these sanctions should only be employed in the context of mutually agreed-upon international procedures. Moreover, temporary trade restrictions used under such exceptional circumstances should consist solely of measures that work through market mechanisms (such as import surcharges) rather than of quantitative restrictions (such as quotas).

3. *Capital Movements*

The role of international capital movements has increased enormously during the last decade and a half. A major share of such flows has been linked to trade and longer-term investment transactions. This even holds true for various types of capital flows that are classified as short-term but that are in fact directly associated with more basic activities. Indeed, trade and capital transactions are often so closely interrelated that it makes no sense to subject them to entirely different rules.

We believe that apart from the special case of certain types of short-term capital movements discussed below, the rules governing restraints on trade and on capital transactions for balance-of-payments reasons should generally be comparable and that every effort should be made to reduce or eliminate such restrictions. We specifically applaud the recent announcement by the U.S. government that existing controls over credit and capital outflows from the United States are to be phased out by the end of 1974.

We also believe that it should generally prove possible to achieve compatibility in countries' goals with respect to their balance-of-payments structures by relying on cooperative international measures that serve to liberalize rather than restrict direct investments and other basic transactions. Efforts to develop positive approaches in these areas (such as reductions in capital outflow restrictions by surplus countries) require high priority in future economic negotiations.

Special problems can, of course, arise in connection with massive and sudden shifts of short-term capital funds. To a considerable extent, such large-scale movements have tended to be a symptom of a more deep-seated lack of confidence in the monetary system and the viability of existing exchange rate relationships. As payments imbalances are reduced and monetary arrangements are strengthened, confidence will be restored and the magnitude of these movements is likely to subside. More frequent exchange parity changes, wider exchange rate margins, and greater use of floats should do much to help deter such flows.

Nevertheless, special measures may still be required at times to deal with very large-scale movements of short-term funds, particularly in the case of countries that find it difficult to offset the impact of these flows on domestic monetary conditions. **We believe, however, that resort to direct controls on short-term capital movements—and particularly to quantitative restrictions—should generally be avoided.** Additional means of coping with such movements should be provided through an expansion of the swap network and the eventual establishment of a new special credit facility in the IMF, as discussed below. In some instances, there may be justification for the use of direct measures to affect short-term capital movements and their domestic impact, such as the imposition of special central bank reserve requirements against bank deposits by nonresidents.

The Reserve Mechanism and Convertibility

If the international monetary system is to function properly, future reserve creation must be based on conscious management of international reserves tailored to the world's needs for liquidity and based on multilateral agreement. SDRs are the only reserve asset that is subject to such management and that does not give rise to the confidence problems associated with gold or dollars. **We endorse the view that SDRs should be given increasing importance in the overall international monetary system, with the aim of eventually making them the principal international reserve asset; that they should be the system's formal numeraire, or "unit of account," against which changes in exchange rates or parities are measured;[3] and that they should be freed of many of the operational limitations to which they are now subject. We also urge that gold be assigned**

3/Determination of the value of SDRs relative to national currencies is quite simple under par value regimes but presents complicated technical issues with a system of managed floats. A variety of techniques can be used to deal with this problem. For example, the value of SDRs under a managed float regime might be defined in terms of a trade-weighted or GNP-weighted average of all (or the major) currencies, computed daily or weekly on daily averages. This approach would assure stability in the value of SDRs in terms of the world's currencies, even when currencies have no par value.

**a sharply diminishing role in the international monetary system and that
its monetary role should eventually be abolished entirely.**

Implementation of these recommendations means that the relative
importance of the dollar as a reserve currency should be reduced and that
in time some form of convertibility of the dollar into official reserve
assets should be reestablished. But hasty steps in these directions would
appear neither practicable nor desirable.

Indeed, for the intermediate-term future, dollars and other national currencies will undoubtedly continue to be a major element in
official reserves. Dollars can be expected to remain the most important
currency that monetary authorities use for intervention in exchange markets. For this reason alone, central banks will need to maintain working
balances of dollars that will count as part of their reserves. At the same
time, other national currencies—notably the German mark and the Japanese yen—are likely to gain increased importance as intervention and
transaction currencies and will thus acquire a relatively larger role in
national reserves.

It also appears that establishment of new monetary arrangements
involving restoration of a significant degree of asset convertibility of the
dollar can be considered only at some time in the future when a number
of conditions have been met. These include significant progress toward
eliminating the existing large payments imbalances and reducing the
accumulated overhang of dollars in foreign official reserves that represent
a potential claim on U.S. reserve assets. In the intervening period, it is
likely that the major countries will continue to place primary reliance on
managed floats for adjusting their payments imbalances. With such
floats, conversions of dollars into official U.S. reserve assets will, under
existing arrangements, occur only to the limited degree that the U.S.
authorities intervene in the exchange markets at their option to buy back
dollars.

Over the longer term, however, any exchange rate arrangement
that involves some form of market intervention—i.e., anything other than
a system of purely unmanaged floats—poses the question of whether it
would be desirable to provide for more extensive asset convertibility of
dollars that monetary authorities acquire through exchange market
operations.

**We believe that the United States should cooperate in interna-
tional efforts to develop acceptable procedures for the eventual restora-**

tion of some form of dollar convertibility into official reserve assets. A move in this direction would in fact be in the interest of all countries. It would give other countries the opportunity to receive payment in reserve assets rather than dollars in settlement of U.S. deficits, and it would help the United States to gain greater powers of initiative in changing its exchange rate.

At the same time, however, we strongly recommend against any U.S. agreement to a new convertibility obligation until arrangements have been worked out which will leave no doubt that this obligation can in fact be sustained. We further recommend that the United States insist that a series of key conditions be met before consideration is given to restoration of some form of convertibility of the dollar into other official reserve assets. These conditions should be precisely articulated and should include (1) adequate provisions for improvements of the international adjustment mechanism; (2) satisfactory means of handling the overhang of outstanding official dollar holdings; (3) new procedures for coping with massive movements of funds; and (4) provisions for adequate international reserve allocation to the United States as well as to other countries.

We believe that the problem of the so-called overhang of dollars in foreign official reserves may be less serious than is frequently thought. The magnitude of the problem should diminish significantly once basic confidence in the strength of the dollar—and the underlying willingness to hold dollars—increases and as the impact of the recent exchange rate realignments becomes fully effective. Moreover, the size of the overhang would tend to be further reduced through actions by surplus countries to remove restrictions on investments by their citizens in other nations, including the United States.

Nevertheless, accelerated efforts to develop ways of consolidating at least part of the overhang of dollars in official hands appear desirable. A variety of techniques should be explored in this connection. Although we do not endorse a specific plan, we believe that a number of principles should be followed in conjunction with any consolidation:

First, arrangements for consolidation or restoring convertibility should in general not restrict countries from holding dollars in their official reserves as working balances and for related purposes if they so wish. Special procedures may, however, have to be developed to assure that existing or future dollar holdings by foreign monetary authorities do not prevent the United States from accumulating reserve assets once its payments position moves into surplus.

Second, because progress toward reducing the overhang and restoring some element of official dollar convertibility is in the interest of all countries, any method that might be used for consolidating the overhang should involve an equitable international sharing of the burden with respect to such matters as interest-rate and maintenance-of-value provisions.

Third, any agreement on consolidation or restoring of convertibility must include adequate arrangements for permitting the United States to earn the extra current account surpluses and to receive the added investment inflows that are required to make the necessary transfers possible.

A more serious threat to dollar convertibility than the official overhang could arise from massive shifts in private dollar balances. **To deal with this problem, we recommend the creation of a new IMF lending facility that would be powerful enough to cope with massive movements of funds that might threaten to undermine a new convertibility obligation by the United States or any other country.** Such a facility should be used only to counter severe threats to convertibility and to deter resort to controls; it should not serve as an instrument for preventing adequate exchange rate flexibility. **To assure that the facility would be used only in appropriate situations, its activation should require approval by the Fund's Managing Director.**

Strengthening International Institutions

We recommend that the IMF be reorganized and strengthened to enable it to cope properly with the new responsibilities that it would assume under the proposed reforms. The following changes would be particularly desirable:

1. The level of country representation in the Fund's major decision-making body must be high enough to allow this body to serve without question as the principal continuing focal point for international monetary coordination and management. An appropriate change would be to retain much of the structure of the present Executive Board in terms of size and distribution of country representation but to provide that

member countries substitute top-level officials as their representatives on the Board whenever this seems desirable.

2. The internal structure and working procedures of the Fund should be more clearly directed at highlighting the mutual responsibilities of surplus and deficit countries in the adjustment process.

3. The upgraded IMF Board should make use of special committees that can focus more intensively on functional issues than is possible for the Board as a whole.

4. Procedures should be developed to allow more integrated consideration of the interrelationship of international monetary problems with trade, investment, tax, and related considerations. This integration should be achieved both within the IMF and through better coordination of its activities with those of the General Agreement on Tariffs and Trade (GATT), OECD, and other relevant organizations.

International Monetary Reform and Development Assistance

Appropriate changes in the formula for allocating SDRs should be considered in instances where it may not adequately reflect the liquidity needs of individual countries; this may well call for an increase in SDR allocations to less developed nations. However, we recommend against the establishment of an automatic link between SDR creation and development assistance in any agreement on international monetary reform.* The amount of SDRs issued should not be based on criteria other than liquidity needs and the proper functioning of the international monetary system.

At the same time, we urge that any agreement on international monetary reform be paralleled by a strengthening of multilateral commitments for a more adequate provision of development assistance to the less developed countries, with aid burdens based on appropriate indicators of national economic strength. We further suggest that in-depth consideration of the balance-of-payments relationships between the developed and less developed nations and their implications for the needed flow and form of development assistance become a required feature of the improved IMF procedures on international monetary adjustment.

---

*See Memoranda by MR. LINCOLN GORDON and MR. DAVIDSON SOMMERS, pages 85 and 86.

Chapter Two

The Degree of Flexibility in Exchange Rates

Although the recent past has seen a dramatic shift toward floating exchange rates, the question of how much flexibility or rigidity in exchange rates will be desirable over the longer term has not yet been fully resolved. The choice among exchange rate systems, in turn, will have major significance with regard to the relative roles that will be played by other adjustment instruments in the future monetary system, including domestic economic policies and direct controls on international trade and capital transactions.

To gain perspective on the relative merits of alternative exchange rate regimes over the longer run as well as in the more immediate future, we have found it useful to examine the strengths and weaknesses of two extreme alternatives: (1) a system of completely fixed rates and (2) fully flexible or cleanly "floating" rates.

Payments Adjustment with Fixed Exchange Rates

The workings of a system of rigidly fixed exchange rates can be best understood by considering the process of payments adjustment that takes place *within* a single country or among a group of countries that have a common currency.

In the United States, for example, trade and payments take place freely among different regions. Balance-of-payments problems can and do arise among such regions, for example when a particular region's imports from other parts of the country exceed its exports. But few have proposed to correct these imbalances by establishing differential exchange rates among regions, that is, by creating separate currencies for each region. Instead, the adjustment occurs through movements of money incomes and through induced shifts of labor and capital resources. If a region has a payments deficit, it will experience a net outflow of funds and money incomes will fall. As a result, demand for goods and services by people of the region is likely to decline and help to reduce the deficit. The lower income, in turn, will tend to place a damper on prices and costs. Some workers will leave the region to find better jobs elsewhere, but the lower costs may in time bring into the area new employers who create new exports. Capital movements may also serve to restore payments balance, although this is by no means assured. If there is an excessive expansion of demand in a region, the process will work in the opposite direction.

This system has great advantages. It promotes the integration of the economy into a single market. By allowing capital and labor to move freely to any section of the country, it facilitates active competition and encourages the most efficient allocation of resources.

Even within individual countries, however, payments imbalances can sometimes give rise to protracted distress within particular regions. A well-known example is the prolonged problems encountered by New England when demands for textile goods shifted elsewhere. For the most part such interregional difficulties tend to be overcome through the compensating effects of national fiscal and monetary measures. These include not only the automatic stabilizing effects of the federal income-tax system and of unemployment insurance but also the use of special expenditure programs, such as revenue sharing and regional development assistance.

A fixed rate system *among* independent countries can similarly be conducive to a high degree of economic integration. To the extent that such a system operates without controls, it permits freedom of labor and capital movements; relieves businessmen and traders of uncertainties regarding the value of the currencies in which they deal; and allows them to take full advantage of the economies of scale and efficiencies associated with larger and competitive markets. Moreover, the use of reserves under fixed rates gives a country leeway to draw temporarily on the resources of other countries by running an import surplus. This serves to mitigate the effects of domestic inflationary pressures. It can provide a useful breathing space for letting the effects of anti-inflationary measures take hold.

Given these advantages of fixed exchange rates, why has rigidity in exchange rates been regarded as a major impediment to the proper functioning of the international monetary system? Basically, the explanation is that in a number of important respects, payments adjustment among independent countries clearly differs from adjustment within a single country. Nations, unlike regions, are usually unwilling to permit (and able to prevent) correction of payments imbalances through movements of incomes that can cause domestic inflation or recession, or through completely unrestricted movements of labor or capital. Modern governments generally are strongly committed to domestic policies that seek to achieve both full employment and price stability. They are not prepared to let the balance of payments deter them from following such policies or from exercising some independence in national monetary management. (With rigid exchange rates and complete freedom of capital movements, separate monetary policies are no longer feasible.) The resistance to letting national policies be dominated by factors originating from abroad is greatly reinforced by the fact that no central international fiscal or monetary authority yet exists that can adequately alleviate the burdens of adjustment under a fixed rate regime.

All this has generally meant that fixed exchange rate regimes have not been permitted to operate without interference. Instead, they have usually been accompanied by a variety of direct controls designed to allow some autonomy in national economic policies. Such controls, of course, significantly reduce the scope for economic integration on which the case for fixed exchange rates is fundamentally based. They often merely serve to delay more fundamental adjustments that a change in exchange rates can bring about. Moreover, once confidence in the fixity of an exchange rate comes into question, speculative pressures are reinforced by the fact that the fixed rate regime gives speculators a "one-way" ride: they may gain if the rate is changed in the predicted direction but will suffer little or no loss if it is maintained.

Payments Adjustments with Floating Exchange Rates

At the other end of the spectrum are fully flexible, or "cleanly floating," exchange rates. With such a system, payments imbalances among countries are corrected by changes in relative prices of their currencies rather than through the movements of reserves. This means that the governments involved do not need to be concerned about whether payments imbalances will cause large inflows or outflows of reserves that might exert unwanted effects on domestic monetary conditions. More generally, it means that domestic policies can to a major extent be insulated from international payments considerations. Countries with floating rates are in effect protected against the destabilizing effects of booms or recessions originating elsewhere, and they do not have to accept domestic deflation and increased unemployment as a means of adjustment when their payments positions are in deficit. By the same token, of course, the impact of inflationary disturbances that originate within the country cannot be shifted elsewhere.

The very fact that this system tends to insulate economies from external influences also means that the scope for economic integration among countries is less than under a fixed rate system without controls. Moreover, individual businessmen and financial institutions incur costs as they seek to cope with the uncertainties associated with continuous changes in exchange rates. They may find that the prices at which they purchase and sell goods change more frequently than before, or they may incur costs involved in purchasing forward cover. The extent of such costs, however, need not be very great if actual variations in exchange rates do not turn out to be very large. Moreover, if the system is one in which controls on trade and capital flows are kept to a minimum, its impact on the degree of economic integration among countries might actually prove more favorable than that of a system of fixed exchange rates accompanied by extensive controls.

Although some advocates of floating rates would always insist on "clean" floats, even those who favor fully flexible exchange rates usually concede that there will be cases in which governmental intervention in the exchange market may be desirable or inevitable. One reason is that governments are important buyers and sellers of goods and services for their own account; they are thus bound to enter in exchange markets in some way. More generally, means have to be found to assure that interventions do not work at cross-purposes. Much more important, however, is the fact that most governments are unwilling to allow very wide or erratic swings in exchange rates that will cause domestic resource shifts which they regard as seriously destabilizing or that run counter to their basic economic objectives.

Most countries are not merely concerned about overall balance in their international payments. They also have distinct objectives with regard to their balance-of-payments structure, particularly the relation between current and capital account transactions. Thus, the major industrial countries have generally sought to reach or maintain a surplus in their trade balance or current account. This tends to be regarded as beneficial to domestic employment and aids the politically strong export industries. The fact that these preferences exist does not mean that they are unchangeable or that they always make a great deal of sense. Current account surpluses by industrial countries do perform the desirable function of permitting a net transfer of resources to the less developed nations. But in an age of inflation, many industrial countries may actually be better off by avoiding excessive surpluses and encouraging relatively more imports; and it is clear that not all countries can have trade surpluses simultaneously.

Nevertheless, national preferences regarding the desirable longer-term structure of each country's international payments do exist. As a minimum, most governments like to see some stability in "basic" transactions such as foreign trade and direct investments. If exchange rates are determined purely by market forces, however, they may fluctuate far more than is desirable in terms of achieving such stability in basic transactions. The reason is that over shorter periods large-scale capital movements can have a far more immediate and sizable impact on exchange rates than more basic trade transactions. In turn, the effects of exchange rate changes on some types of capital movements tend to be felt much more quickly than the effects on trade and long-term investment, which may only be fully manifested after several years.

Huge shifts of short-term capital funds can also occur in the modern world purely for reasons of convenience. Other movements may be induced by interest differentials—including those associated with differences in the phasing of the business cycle in different countries—and by speculative considerations. Governments will seek to mitigate the effects of marked swings in exchange rates if they believe these will give excessively large jolts to their economies or work counter to their longer-range structural goals. With flexible rates, they may either seek to intervene in exchange markets or try to achieve their objectives by capital and other controls.

The resistance to full exchange rate flexibility tends to be substantially greater in countries where foreign transactions constitute a relatively high proportion of national economic transactions. It is less serious for countries like the United States where such transactions are a much smaller percentage of total GNP. The desire for more stable exchange rates also tends to be higher among nations that are very active trading partners, such as many of the members of the Common Market. This is why most of these countries recently decided on maintaining relatively stable exchange rates among each other. On the other hand, a joint float between major Common Market members and the United States proved more acceptable because trans-Atlantic trade is much less important than trade within the Market.

Choosing Between Alternative Exchange Rate Systems

Which of these alternative exchange rate systems—fixed or floating —is the more desirable goal toward which policy makers should aim? And what combination of arrangements and policies is most suitable in practice over the nearer-term future?

Paradoxically, both fixed and floating exchange rate regimes constitute desirable longer-term solutions. Among many countries, fixed exchange rate relationships already exist. Thus, smaller countries often find it convenient and attractive to tie their exchange rates to those of larger countries; for example, the parities of many countries in the Western Hemisphere are tied to the dollar. For most advanced countries, however, rigidly fixed rates will probably become appropriate only in the distant future when these countries will in fact be highly integrated and will have established a wide range of common governmental functions. Even within the Common Market, it is likely to take a considerable time before such a degree of cohesion can be attained.

Over the foreseeable future, however, rigidly fixed exchange rates clearly cannot resolve the problems that currently exist or are bound to arise among the major trading countries. For these countries, the more desirable course in the nearer-term future will be a considerably greater degree of exchange rate flexibility than has existed until very recently.

In the past, many businessmen and financiers were among the strongest opponents of more flexible exchange rates because of their belief that they would create excessive uncertainty in economic transactions and interfere with rational profit calculations. After years of experience with successive exchange market crises and increasing controls under fixed rate arrangements, this is no longer the dominant view.

We have given careful consideration to the impact of relatively greater exchange flexibility on our own business operations, including trade and financial transactions as well as direct investments overseas. In general, we have concluded that increased flexibility in exchange rates will not be a serious detriment to business operations and investments, *provided* it occurs in conjunction with a reduction in arbitrary governmental controls and interferences with particular transactions. The important matter from the point of view of business is to be able to make rational forward plans. Uncertainties created by the difficulties of trying to anticipate ad hoc governmental decisions and the vagaries of the administration of controls can often be substantially more serious than uncertainties created by seeking to cope with evolving situations in financial markets that are governed mainly by the free interplay of demand and supply. In general, we prefer to deal with predictions of market forces rather than governmental actions. Moreover, when capital controls are minimized, effective futures markets in foreign exchange can develop that will allow businessmen to cover themselves against the risks of excessive future rate fluctuations.

This does not mean that we welcome wide swings in exchange rates. But greater exchange rate flexibility need not involve larger de facto changes in rates. Indeed, we consider it likely that once confidence in the strength of the international monetary system is restored, the scope for greater flexibility in rates will lead to smaller actual variations in such rates than have occurred in the past. To be sure, views in this area are not unanimous. Thus, the possibility cannot be dismissed that over time speculation under floating rates will, on balance, prove destabilizing. But this is an empirical question that will only be resolved as experience under the new system of floating rates accumulates.

We realize, of course, that the type of system that would be acceptable from the viewpoint of American business and the United States as a whole may not be equally suited to the needs of all other countries. Hence, we agree with Secretary Shultz's view that the new international monetary system must allow individual countries a wide range of choice with respect to the adjustment techniques they find most suitable to meet their needs. Obviously, however, exchange rate systems are two-sided affairs, and their design must be worked out in a cooperative fashion. The important point is that all countries must be under strong compulsion to bring about adjustments more promptly than in the past and in ways that call for a minimum of artificial restraints on free market forces.

Requirements for an Improved Exchange Rate System

The realistic prospect is that any feasible exchange rate system for the intermediate-term future will involve a limited degree of flexibility. We believe that as this system evolves, the differences between those who favor a relatively high degree of reliance on floating exchange rates and those who prefer par values with more frequent and smaller adjustments are not likely to appear as important as in the past. As already noted, those who believe in a freely floating system of exchange rates as a norm will admit that intervention by governments is likely to be necessary on various occasions. On the other hand, those who favor a system of periodic but frequent adjustments in par values are now generally also amenable to allowing temporary floats. Thus, the two approaches may in fact tend to converge.

For these reasons, we do not consider it essential that a decision be made now on the precise future admixture between reliance on floats and on adjustable parities. Indeed, there are advantages in keeping options open. The more important requirements, in our view, are the following:

1. **Exchange rate changes must henceforth play a substantially larger role in balance-of-payments adjustment than was the case under the Bretton Woods regime.** They should no longer be the adjustment instrument of last resort. In many instances, to be sure, other policy instruments will still need to play a key role in such adjustments (see discussion in Chapter Three). **There should, however, be a presumption that exchange rate changes will normally be used to assist in the correction of**

payments imbalances, either as the instrument that is most appropriate in particular circumstances or as a second line of defense to be used promptly if other methods do not give evidence that they can achieve the needed correction within a fairly brief period of time.

2. **The essential needs of sound international trade and finance can be met either by (a) a system of floating exchange rates involving periodic official intervention or (b) exchange parities subject to frequent and relatively small adjustments, with provisions for wider margins and options for temporary floats under appropriate circumstances.** Regardless of which system is adopted, however, it will be of key importance to have a clear set of internationally agreed-upon rules governing the operation of the system.

3. **To the extent that par values are retained, exchange rate margins between the United States and other major countries should be somewhat wider than was provided under the Smithsonian Agreement.** This would not prevent other countries, such as those within the European Community, from maintaining different margins among each other if they considered this desirable. A further widening of exchange margins vis-à-vis other major countries should assist in reducing the scope for destabilizing capital movements. It would increase the risks of exchange losses for speculators and diminish possible gains from movements of funds in response to international interest-rate differentials.

4. **Under either type of exchange rate regime, international agreement is needed to assure that the use of direct controls on trade and capital transactions is kept to a minimum. More generally, better international understandings are required with respect to the appropriate use of different types of adjustment instruments under different circumstances.**

5. **The application and enforcement of all these rules requires a strong central authority. We believe that this authority should principally be lodged in a strengthened International Monetary Fund.**

Developing Rules for Intervention and Adjustment

In most respects, the same basic types of considerations should govern the design of rules for floating rates with intervention and for par value regimes with provisions for frequent parity adjustments.

1. A variety of cooperative arrangements is clearly needed to assure that the actions of national authorities do not work at cross-purposes. This need is most obvious in connection with official interventions in "floating" markets or within relatively wide margins around agreed-upon parities. In these cases, there is little time for extended discussion of what should be done once the markets have opened. Thus, prior understandings and presumptive rules regarding the extent and nature of permissible intervention will generally be required, although some scope for consultation in specific instances would remain.

With adjustable par values, greater scope exists for prior consultation on coordination of the timing and nature of adjustment actions. But more adequate procedures than those used in the past are needed to assure that such coordination actually occurs.

In the case of wider bands, consideration should be given to the creation of an "inner band" within which intervention would be ruled out altogether. This would help to discourage currency speculation.

2. One category of rules will have to relate to the magnitude and speed of adjustment actions. In the case of floating rates, such rules should generally be designed to guard against overly frequent or sizable interventions. Some smoothing of exchange rate movements would be permitted in order to prevent unduly large and erratic swings in rates. Intervention would also be appropriate in the event of "runaway" or "disorderly" market conditions involving very rapid rate movements in one direction or massive flows of funds. But presumptive rules would have to be established to prohibit intervention unless the amplitude or speed of changes in rates exceeds specified limits. Prior agreement might also be possible to offset unsettling effects of particular types of transactions.

With adjustable par values, the rules would mainly be concerned with assuring that parity changes and other adjustment actions occur with sufficient frequency and in large enough magnitude. **We favor the use of objective indicators to establish international presumption of the need for adjustment action. Such indicators should focus mainly on the results of inadequate adjustment, notably excessively large or deficient international reserve positions.** If a reserve test is used, however, we would favor emphasis on the *speed* of changes in reserves as well as on the extent of deviations from appropriate reserve levels. Moreover, actual decisions on the need for corrective action and the type of action to be taken would have to take account of a range of considerations in addition to the behavior of reserves.

3. With either partially controlled floating rates or frequently adjustable par values, rules are needed to prevent countries from using the international adjustment mechanism as a device for unfairly shifting the burden of their internal business-cycle problems to other nations. (In fact, even with cleanly floating rates, there may be a need to deal with the effects of capital movements triggered by cyclically induced interest rate differentials.) This means that countries should not be allowed to use exchange rate depreciations to strengthen their export markets in order to shift unemployment to their trading partners. It also means that countries should not be permitted to defer parity changes when this results in an undue spreading of their internal inflationary pressures to other countries.

4. Another category of rules would have to relate to the nature and extent of actions that countries might be permitted to take in order to achieve specific objectives with respect to the structure of their balance of payments. Basically, this requires some continuing international consultation on the best ways of reconciling conflicting balance-of-payments aims of different countries with respect to their need for trade and current account surpluses and the extent of long-term capital inflows. More specifically, it calls for understandings regarding the extent to which proper domestic economic policies and exchange rate adjustments should be permitted to be supplemented by various types of direct controls on trade and capital movements. The considerations that should enter into such understandings are more fully discussed in Chapter Three.

Chapter Three

Choosing Among
Adjustment Instruments

We have indicated our belief that the future international monetary system should place substantially greater reliance on relatively frequent exchange rate adjustments than was the case under the Bretton Woods regime. We have also stressed, however, that greater flexibility in exchange rates will not solve all adjustment problems and that reliance on other measures would still be required. This chapter focuses on the appropriate roles of different instruments of adjustment in different situations, including the role of exchange rates, domestic policies, and measures directly affecting trade and capital movements.

How Effective Are Exchange Rate Changes?

It is paradoxical that at the very time when exchange rate changes have become much more frequent and floating rates much more general, widespread public doubts have emerged about whether exchange rates adjustments will actually be of significant assistance in eliminating basic payments imbalances. These doubts have, in part, had their origin in disappointment over the fact that evidence of beneficial responses to the exchange rate adjustments under the Smithsonian Agreement has emerged much more slowly than had widely been expected. The doubts have been reinforced by a belief that structural changes in international trade and other economic relations are rendering international economic transactions increasingly less responsive to relative cost and price changes and thus to parity adjustments.

Two questions need to be raised in this connection. First, how responsive are international trade and other current account transactions to changes in exchange rates? Second, what are the implications for policy if the average speed and degree of such responsiveness should prove to be significantly less than has been assumed?

Economic Responses to Exchange Rate Changes. There is evidence that a number of factors are at work which may tend to make trade among the major industrial countries less price-responsive in the coming decades than in the past. These factors appear to be particularly important in the case of the United States. Thus, the current energy shortage is bound to result in increased American dependence on oil imports over the medium-term future. A depreciation in exchange rates that increases the effective prices of petroleum products for American purchasers will not necessarily reduce their demand for such products, so that the exchange rate adjustment is likely to result in larger rather than reduced payments to foreign suppliers.

It is also true that important types of American exports, such as agricultural products, are in short supply abroad and that many of the high-technology items that the United States sells are not available elsewhere. Thus, purchasers of these products may not change the volume of their purchases significantly in response to price reductions. Another factor that tends to reduce price responsiveness in international trade is the use of quantitative trade restrictions by many countries. Finally, payments associated with defense deployments abroad can hardly be expected to be very responsive to exchange rate changes.*

The existence of these tendencies and exceptions, however, by no means indicates that exchange rate changes will not exert very significant net effects on international payments positions, although these effects will often be felt only after a substantial time lag.

---

*See Memorandum by MR. HERMAN L. WEISS, page 87.

One reason for this is that a great many international economic transactions will undoubtedly continue to show a high responsiveness to changes in exchange rates. For many individual products, prices do make an important difference to the ultimate purchaser. Imports of foreign automobiles, for example, have clearly slackened since the U.S. exchange adjustment made their price tags relatively higher than those of comparable domestic cars. Similarly, many American tourists can be expected to change future plans to travel to foreign countries if they find that exchange rate revaluations have raised costs in these countries appreciably. And although the immediate demand for foreign oil products may not necessarily diminish as the price of these products rises, there will be greater incentives to develop alternative domestic energy sources (such as coal) that have now become relatively cheaper.

In the case of the United States, the value of goods moving in foreign trade still consists to a very substantial degree of items for which demand is responsive to relative price changes, such as many durable and nondurable goods and a large number of semi-manufactured products. A devaluation, therefore, can be expected to have a considerable effect on the trade balance. This is true not only because price changes may influence the overall demand for many of these products but also because the change in relative prices tends to result in a significant amount of switching of purchases from foreign to domestic sources. Moreover, changes in relative international prices can bring products into the export market that had previously not been competitive at all.

It is also important to recognize that exchange rate changes affect relative costs and will therefore exert effects on the behavior of *suppliers* as well as of purchasers. In instances where an exchange rate adjustment fails to result in changed prices of a particular product, it will still tend to affect the profits of the supplier. For example, an exporter in a country that revalues will find his profit margins squeezed if he maintains his prices in the foreign market because the value of the foreign currency in which he is paid is now less than before. This will tend to make him less eager to promote sales of his product in the foreign country concerned and in time will cause him to shift his sales efforts to the domestic market or to other areas.

The best evidence available indicates that in earlier instances of significant exchange rate adjustments, the trade balances of the countries in question did respond to a substantial degree. This was, for instance, the case after the French devaluations of 1958 and 1969, after the Canadian devaluation of 1962, and after the British devaluation of 1967. Conversely, the revaluation of the mark in 1969 appears to have reduced Germany's trade surplus below what it otherwise would have been.

Exchange rate changes can also affect the volume of new direct investment. To the extent that the recent dollar devaluations have rendered U.S. products more competitive, both in export markets and in relation to imports, it should become more attractive for foreigners to establish manufacturing and other operations in the United States. This will be particularly true in cases where U.S. operations constitute an alternative to direct exports from abroad. However, apart from the effects of improved international competitiveness, the rates of return on new investments will not be affected, since the exchange rate adjustment has comparable effects on the funds invested and the funds earned.

Conclusive evidence regarding the effects of the exchange rate adjustments initiated at the Smithsonian meeting and later is not yet available. It was to be expected that the initial responses would be the opposite of those desired. Thus, higher total payments had to be made for imports already on order; effects of the devaluation in reducing orders would only show up later, as new orders were placed. But the time lags involved have been greater than many people anticipated. Moreover, the differential phasing of the business cycle in the United States and abroad has been strongly adverse to an improvement in the U.S. payments situation, thus offsetting part of the favorable influence of relative price changes. These factors, together with the special problems associated with the energy shortage, have delayed a favorable impact of the recent dollar devaluations on the U.S. trade situation. It remains likely, however, that the eventual effects will be substantial.

Policy Implications. Nevertheless, it may turn out to be true that correction of payments imbalances through exchange rate adjustments will be a more difficult and prolonged process in the future than has been the case in the past. Does this imply, as has been suggested by many of those who question the efficacy of exchange rates, that reliance on exchange rate flexibility should largely be abandoned? The answer, in our view, is clearly "No."

It is true that appropriate domestic demand and structural policies can and should in many cases play a key role in restoring the competitive positions and payments balances of individual countries. As is indicated later in this statement, such policies can serve to increase a country's welfare, even under fully flexible exchange rates. But there are important instances when the domestic and international policy requirements are in conflict and when proper domestic policies measures cannot be expected to resolve the payments problem.

In these cases, the real alternative to reliance on exchange rate adjustments consists of the use of various types of direct restraints. To the extent that such restraints work through the price mechanism—as, for example, in the case of import surcharges—they are subject to essentially the same drawbacks as changes in exchange rates. Import surcharges alone, moreover, are inferior to exchange rate variations as an adjustment device because they do not affect exports or non-trade transactions. Indeed, when imported goods are used to produce export items, the competitiveness of exports can actually be harmed by such surcharges. Moreover, exchange markets have in the past usually interpreted the imposition of import surcharges as a prelude to a general devaluation. The other major alternative is the imposition of quantitative restrictions, particularly the use of import or export quotas. Such devices, however, are highly undesirable over the longer run because of the damage they inflict on efficient resource allocations. Over time, quotas are likely to increase rather than reduce imbalances in the payments position of deficit countries because they add to cost-push pressures and stimulate inflation.

Thus, any finding that exchange rate changes affect current account transactions with a longer lag and to a lesser degree than previously anticipated does not mean that reliance on such changes should be sharply curtailed. Quite the contrary, it tends to imply that relatively greater rather than lesser use of exchange rate changes may have to be made in the future and that the changes have to be initiated sooner than has usually been the case in the past. It also indicates the need for more vigorous actions to remove structural impediments to price flexibility and the proper functioning of competitive market forces.

The Role of Domestic Economic Policies

In popular discussions, the impression is sometimes conveyed that with increased exchange rate flexibility, pursuit of appropriate domestic economic policies will cease to be of any importance as far as a country's international economic position is concerned. Such a view is based on a serious misconception.

It is true that with freely floating exchange rates, a country's over-all balance-of-payments position will be brought into equilibrium whether or not it follows prudent domestic policies. Moreover, floating rates largely protect a country from the effects of inflation or deflation originating abroad. They also mean that the country does not have to accept increased unemployment as a remedy for a balance-of-payments deficit.

But it does not follow that inappropriate domestic economic policies inflict no damage on the nation's international economic relations. Quite to the contrary, both with relatively fixed and with highly flexible exchange rates, sound management of domestic economic policies will in a majority of situations be of key importance for a country's relative strength in the international economy.

In the case of relatively fixed exchange rates, the importance of proper domestic policies relates mainly to so-called non-dilemma situations, in which policies needed to achieve domestic economic objectives also serve to reduce imbalances in the external payments position. Thus, when a country suffers from domestic demand and cost inflation as well as a payments deficit, policies to curtail excessive spending and control costs will be appropriate on both domestic and international grounds. A failure to come to grips with the inflation will lead to a further deterioration in the country's payments position. To be sure, some part of the problem can be temporarily shifted to other countries, because the increased imports induced by the high levels of demand will add to domestic supplies and help to hold prices down. But this safety valve provides only limited relief, exhausts the country's reserves and credit resources, and eventually generates intense domestic demands for increased protection.

With relatively flexible exchange rates, domestic demand and cost inflation that is relatively greater than elsewhere will be fully felt at home and will lead to prompt depreciation of the value of the country's currency. This will reduce the welfare of its citizens by making it more costly for them to acquire foreign goods and services. (Of course, if a fixed rate system protects an inappropriate rate through widespread controls, there may be an even greater loss in welfare if certain goods cannot be purchased at all.) Moreover, improvement in the country's competitive international position that an exchange depreciation is intended to achieve will be frustrated unless strong measures are taken to prevent an accelerating domestic inflationary spiral. Nor will an exchange rate adjustment be likely to induce a sizable influx of new investment to a depreciating country if its internal economic policies are basically unsound.

We cannot emphasize too strongly, therefore, that regardless of the particular type of exchange rate regime that may be used, sound domestic fiscal and monetary policies will continue to be of fundamental importance for the maintenance of healthy international economic and monetary relationships. This is especially true in the case of the United States because the acceptability of the dollar continues to rest in major part on the confidence that foreign dollar holders place in the strength and stability of the American economy. In particular, we consider it vitally important that (1) fiscal and monetary policies be vigorously used to prevent an excessive U.S. demand expansion, (2) major reforms in Congressional and Executive Branch budget procedures be adopted promptly so that total government spending can be brought under effective control, (3) wage-price restraint be forcefully applied to help bring cost-push pressures under control to the extent that they can be effectively used to supplement adequate fiscal and monetary measures,* and (4) major new efforts be undertaken by government, business, labor, and the farm sector to achieve a wide range of structural reforms that will make the economy more competitive and productive along lines recommended in our July 1972 statement on *High Employment Without Inflation.*

It is true that proper domestic policies will not improve a country's international position in so-called dilemma cases, that is, those in which domestic and international objectives conflict, such as internal deflation and a payments deficit. In many of these cases, the correct solution is an exchange rate adjustment that will leave the country free to pursue its legitimate domestic goals. But in the greater number of actual situations, proper domestic economic policies can be a major factor in solving the country's international problems, either in conjunction with some flexibility in exchange rates or as an alternative to the use of exchange rate adjustments. Reliance on domestic measures can be especially important in cases where the effects of exchange rate changes tend to be relatively weak or long delayed.*

There are also numerous domestic structural measures that can help to correct more basic imbalances in a country's payments position.

---

*See Memorandum by MR. JOHN D. HARPER, page 83.

Measures to increase productivity, actions to eliminate unnecessary subsidies, and the use of incomes policies can all serve to strengthen a country's international competitive position. In other cases, improvements in monetary policy instruments can make the country's monetary system less vulnerable to large inflows of volatile funds from abroad. Other types of structural measures are needed to deal with long-range problems on which current exchange rate movements may have little effect. A prime example involves the enormous potential threat to the payments position of the United States and of other industrial countries that stems from the growing energy shortages and the dramatic rise in international reserve accumulations by oil producing countries in the Middle East. These issues will have to be handled by a wide variety of special measures, including steps to increase domestic U.S. energy sources and expand opportunities for capital investment by the oil producing countries. This will require a series of cooperative actions by all the developed countries.

Trade Policies and the Adjustment Process

In recent years, measures directly affecting the trade account—such as import surcharges, export subsidies, quantitative trade restrictions and various other devices—have frequently been used as a means of affecting a country's trade and payments position. What role, if any, should such measures play in the future, when the scope for flexibility in exchange rates will presumably be far greater than it was in the past?

Clearly, trade policy and balance-of-payments adjustment policies are closely interrelated. Thus, trade liberalization measures that are based on reciprocal concessions by different countries may not be successful if the balance-of-payments adjustment process fails to produce a rough overall balance between changes in exports and in imports. The problem is that reciprocal concessions with respect to the levels of particular tariffs may have different quantitative impacts on actual purchases in different countries. If the overall imbalances become too large, the country whose trade position worsens may suffer increased unemployment and face greater demands for trade protection, thus jeopardizing all efforts to pursue a liberal trade policy.

In turn, the possibilities for effective adjustment through exchange rate changes and through domestic policy coordination can be significantly influenced by trade policies. Parity changes operate through the price and cost mechanism. Their effects can be sharply blunted or even negated when trade restrictions distort that mechanism, for example, when quantitative trade restrictions such as import quotas keep foreign buyers from increasing the total volume of their purchases in response to an effective price decline associated with a devaluation. The extensive import quotas of Japan and the Common Agricultural Policy of the European Community are key instances of restrictive trade practices that have impeded better payments adjustment. By the same token, efforts to facilitate adjustment through exchange rate changes call for comprehensive steps to dismantle nontariff and other trade barriers that work counter to the proper functioning of market forces.

We consider it essential, therefore, that international monetary and trade negotiations be closely coordinated so that trade liberalization and improved monetary adjustment will be able to progress in parallel.

Separate questions arise when trade measures are themselves used as significant instruments of adjustment. There is much to be said for using unilateral reductions of trade barriers by surplus countries as an adjustment device. Such reductions can help to promote a freer world economy, although they should not be used as an excuse for deferring needed parity adjustments. But the use of new trade restrictions for purposes of balance-of-payments adjustment is normally open to serious objections and is basically inferior to exchange rate changes.

In an earlier policy statement,[1] we indicated that under some circumstances, countries in balance-of-payments difficulties should be permitted the option of "the temporary use of special border tax adjustments or equivalent import surcharges and export subsidies at uniform rates." However, one of the principal earlier arguments for the employment of such weapons—that the United States, unlike other countries, cannot take the initiative in changing its exchange rate—is today no longer valid. As already noted, moreover, it makes no sense to resort to import surcharges on the ground that these would be more effective than exchange rate changes in producing adjustment.

Therefore, import surcharges and similar measures should not be a substitute for needed exchange rate realignments. We believe that it would be a serious mistake for the United States or other countries to

---

[1] *Nontariff Distortions of Trade,* A Statement on National Policy by the Research and Policy Committee, Committee for Economic Development (New York: Sept. 1969).

superimpose import surcharges, extensive quantitative trade restrictions, or export subsidies on top of appropriate exchange rate changes as a means of dealing with overall payments adjustment. To the extent that adjustment techniques with a differential effect on current and capital account transactions may be called for, measures other than trade restrictions would seem preferable, as is discussed in the next section.

There is one special situation, however, in which reliance on trade measures in a balance-of-payments adjustment context may be justified, but only under international agreement and surveillance.

Thus, it may be appropriate to authorize uniform import surcharges as an ultimate sanction against a country or countries that fail to take proper action to curb excessive payments surpluses. The U.S. government should have legislative authority to make use of such measures. But these sanctions should only be employed in the context of mutually agreed-upon international procedures. In any event, if temporary trade restrictions are used under these exceptional circumstances, they should consist solely of measures that work through market mechanisms (such as import surcharges) rather than of quantitative restrictions (such as quotas). The fact that quotas are the only trade instrument that can be used for adjustment under GATT rules clearly indicates that these rules need to be changed. Moreover, before sanctions are imposed, every effort should be made to utilize penalties that are less disruptive—for example those that are primarly financial in nature, such as reductions of new SDR allocations or a tax on the country's excess reserve holdings.

Measures to Affect Capital Movements

The role of capital movements in the adjustment process has increased enormously since the time of the Bretton Woods Agreement, particularly within the last decade and a half. Such movements now account for a larger volume of international payments than trade transactions. One element in this increase has been the growth of direct investment. About 10 per cent of world output represents production by national and multinational firms in foreign countries; and U.S. foreign direct investment alone increased more than sevenfold from 1950 to 1971. The closely connected rise of multinational firms, which now account for about one-half of nonagricultural international trade, has been a major element in fostering closer integration of world capital and money markets and in accelerating international economic integration generally.

At the same time, there has been an almost explosive increase in the available pool of short-term liquid assets that can move rapidly across international borders. For example, total deposits in the Eurocurrency market alone have recently been estimated at $80 to $100 billion or more, with increases in deposit volume at least partly fueled by bank credit creation. Only a fraction of these private funds is actually available for speculation, but the potential for disruptive influences from these sources has clearly become enormous.

This great expansion in capital flows was partly made possible by the progressive dismantling of many of the controls that had existed in the earlier postwar years. However, the succession of payments crises has led to numerous new capital restrictions since then. Particularly in the past several years the new restrictions were introduced in association with the use of more flexible exchange rates and currency floats.

Although the Bretton Woods rules called for the greatest possible freedom in trade and other current trade account transactions, they indicated that direct restrictions on capital movements for balance-of-payments reasons were permissible and sometimes desirable. In our view, a general distinction of this type is no longer acceptable under modern conditions. Trade and direct investment transactions, for example, are often so closely interlinked that it makes no sense to subject them to entirely different rules in a balance-of-payments context.[2] **We believe that apart from the special case of certain types of short-term capital movements, the rules governing restraints on trade and on capital transactions for balance-of-payments reasons should generally be comparable and that every effort should be made to reduce or eliminate such restrictions.** We specifically applaud the recent announcement by the U.S. government that existing controls over credit and capital outflows from the United States are to be phased out by the end of 1974.

Direct investment and other longer-term capital flows. Restrictions on foreign investment and other types of longer-term capital movements frequently arise from a desire to prevent foreign ownership

---

2/The issue of differential treatment of foreign investment for reasons not connected with the balance-of-payments situation is discussed in the next section.

or control of particular industries rather than from broader balance-of-payments considerations. Questions of discrimination against foreign investment through direct controls, fiscal devices, and other methods should be made subject to clear-cut and consistent international rules. We welcome the current efforts within the OECD to develop procedures of this type.

In many other instances, however, governmental actions to control or influence direct investment and other longer-term capital transactions have reflected a more general concern with maintaining or achieving a desired structure in a country's balance of payments, that is, a particular division between the current and the capital account. This aim will not necessarily be accomplished by floating rates or by other methods that merely bring the overall balance-of-payments accounts into equilibrium. From the viewpoint of many European countries, for example, it makes a major difference whether the U.S. payments position is brought into overall balance through (a) the development of a very large U.S. trade surplus that would permit a massive further increase in American direct investment in Europe or (b) a reduced net flow of such investments to Europe paralleled by a much more modest improvement in the U.S. trade position.

Although we believe that ultimately the payments structures of different countries should be largely determined by market forces, we recognize that the actions of most major nations will in fact be influenced by their implicit targets regarding current and capital account transactions. **We are convinced, however, that it should generally prove possible to achieve consistency in national goals for payments structures by relying on cooperative international measures that serve to liberalize rather than restrict direct investments and other basic transactions. In our view, efforts to develop positive approaches in these areas require high priority in future economic negotiations.** Many surplus countries, for example, can take measures to reduce restrictions on capital outflows. It is also encouraging that the U.S. government has recently agreed to explore possible actions to remove inhibitions in the inflow of capital into the United States.

Short-term capital flows. As a result of the unprecedented flows of funds across exchanges that were associated with the recent currency crises, it has become popular to view all these flows as speculative in nature and as major causes of instability in the system. Such a view ignores the complex character of international capital movements and the diversity of the factors affecting them. Capital flows generally classified as "short-term" often finance international trade or longer-run investments (as in the case of working capital requirements) and are therefore directly related to the uses to which real resources are put. To a major extent, the recent massive flows of short-term funds (including those stemming from "leads and lags" in payments for current transactions) have been a symptom rather than a fundamental cause of instability. They were triggered by, and then fed upon, a lack of confidence in a given set of exchange parities and in the willingness and ability of governments to maintain these parities. Clearly, therefore, by far the most important means of coping with the problem of excessive movements of capital must be the establishment of a monetary system and an international adjustment mechanism that command the confidence of the private markets.

Of course, to the extent that massive movements of short-term funds do take place, they can in certain situations create significant problems for the monetary system. Such flows may seriously impair the ability of individual countries to carry out independent monetary policies because many countries do not have sufficient means to offset fully the effect of large capital inflows on their domestic money supplies. Moreover, excessively volatile capital movements may lead to much wider swings in market exchange rates under either par value or floating rate systems than are desirable for trade and other basic transactions.

Unfortunately, the reaction of a number of foreign governments in the recent currency crises has been to impose new controls on capital movements. Apart from the fact that such controls simply are not very effective, treating symptoms by means of controls rather than attacking the more fundamental problems directly is a course that seems unlikely to promote greater stability in the system.

We believe that resort to direct controls on short-term capital movements—and particularly resort to quantitative restrictions—should generally be avoided.

a. Greater use of currency floats may by itself significantly lessen the likelihood of excessive swings in short-term capital movements since speculators' risks are greatly increased. Only experience, however, will indicate whether markets will in fact behave in this fashion or whether floats might actually encourage destabilizing speculation.

b. With par value systems, excessive volatility in capital flows should be discouraged by reliance on wider margins and on relatively frequent but small parity adjustments. Under such arrangements, speculators often stand to lose more from changes in rates within the margins than they can gain from correctly anticipating parity changes.

c. Excessive shifts of funds in response to international interest rate differentials can be further reduced by improved coordination of national economic policies, particularly in the monetary area. Countries should not be expected to pursue monetary policies that run counter to their domestic goals, but they do have scope for cooperation in such matters as the timing of policy changes and the mix between using fiscal and monetary instruments.

d. Central bank mutual credit facilities or "swap" arrangements can be (and recently have been) enlarged to help offset the payments effects of unusually wide swings in the movement of short-term private funds that are likely to be reversed within relatively brief periods of time. Eventually, however, swap facilities should be replaced by the proposed special lending facility in the IMF.

e. A panoply of techniques should be used to defuse the destabilizing potential of the Eurocurrency market, including withdrawal of central bank funds from this market and application of special reserve or predeposit requirements. In addition, the major countries might on appropriate occasions undertake joint open-market operations in the Eurodollar market.

Even if all these various approaches are employed, a case may remain for some measures that affect short-term capital movements more directly; this is particularly true for special measures to reduce the impact of such movements on domestic monetary conditions in certain countries. But in these instances, preference should be given to the use of central banking incentives and disincentives that involve minimum interference with market processes, such as special reserve requirements against bank deposits by nonresidents or the use of negative interest rates. Moreover, every effort should be made to subject such measures to multilateral surveillance and to apply them in the context of international coordination. In many cases, for example, countries may agree that it would be to their mutual benefit to concentrate on measures to prevent undesired *inflows* of capital rather than on actions affecting outflows.

We also believe that restraints that discriminate as little as possible among individual types of transactions tend to be superior to those that do discriminate. Thus, if differential treatment of current and capital account transactions is sought, the use of dual exchange market systems is likely to be preferable to restrictions on individual categories of trade or capital flows. However, reliance on dual exchange rates should not become an excuse for delaying needed overall exchange rate adjustments or be encouraged as a general practice. Such systems are hard to maintain once the differential between the two rates exceeds certain limits. Moreover, the types of controls that are needed to make the system work are far more difficult to apply in some countries than in others.

For the longer run, the solution to dealing with excessive swings in short-term capital movements should include two basic reforms that are more fully discussed in Chapter Four: the consolidation into longer-term investments of the overhang of unwanted dollars in official hands and the establishment of a special new credit facility in the IMF.

Chapter Four

The Reserve Mechanism and Convertibility

Major improvements in the balance-of-payments adjustment process are clearly essential for the proper functioning of the international monetary system. However, they will not be effective unless adequate mechanisms are also available to assure that the volume and growth of international monetary reserves will be properly adapted to underlying liquidity needs.

The overall need for international reserves, in turn, depends to a significant degree on the character and efficiency of the adjustment process. To the extent that improved adjustment procedures succeed in reducing the magnitude of payments imbalances, the world's requirements for official reserves will be less than would otherwise be the case. In fact, if adjustment were to be based solely on "cleanly floating" exchange rates, there would be relatively little need for governments to draw on their official international reserves. Clearly, current estimates of future international reserve needs will have to take careful account of the evolving changes in adjustment techniques.

As indicated earlier, however, governments are not likely to give up entirely the management of their exchange rate systems. Even with floating rates, they can be expected to intervene in exchange markets on various occasions. Thus, international reserves will continue to play an important role.

Moving Toward SDRs as the Primary Reserve Asset

There are three principal forms in which nations hold international reserves at the present time: gold, foreign exchange (mainly in the form of dollars) and IMF Special Drawing Rights. A fourth and less significant reserve category consists of reserve positions in the IMF that countries acquire as a result of gold subscriptions to the Fund and as a by-product of regular IMF operations.

As Table 2 indicates, the relative importance of the different types of reserve assets has shifted sharply during the post-World War II period. In 1945 gold accounted for over two-thirds of total international reserves, and foreign exchange accounted for the remainder. By 1960 these proportions had changed only moderately, although the percentage of dollars in total foreign exchange holdings had nearly doubled. However, by 1969 gold had dropped to 50 per cent of total international reserves and foreign exchange holdings were over 40 per cent. During this period, Special Drawing Rights did not exist; they were not authorized until 1968 and were first issued in 1970.

Between 1969 and 1972, the volume and composition of international reserves changed even more dramatically. Total international reserves nearly doubled, a far larger percentage increase than was recorded during the entire period from 1945 to 1969. Although the amount of gold holdings remained relatively unchanged, there was an almost four-fold increase in foreign holdings of dollars. By the end of 1972, gold constituted only one-quarter of total international reserves; dollar and other foreign exchange holdings accounted for over two-thirds of the total; and the newly created SDRs aggregated 6 per cent.

The experience underlying these statistics made it increasingly clear that neither gold nor dollars could provide a really satisfactory basis for supplying needed additions to total international reserves. The availability of gold for monetary purposes is affected by numerous factors that are unrelated to the needs of the international monetary system, for example, the uncertain pace of new gold discoveries and the demand for gold for nonmonetary purposes. Moreover, in addition to serving as an international monetary reserve, gold is traded in a relatively thin private commodity market in which monetary authorities have generally agreed not to intervene and in which prices can fluctuate sharply. This has raised

Table 2: International Monetary Reserves 1945, 1960, 1969 and 1972

Billions of Dollars				
	1945	*1960*	*1969*	*1972*
Total Gold Reserves	33.3	38.0	39.1	38.8
U.S. Reserves	20.1	17.8	11.9	10.5
Foreign Exchange	14.3	18.6	32.4	101.7
U.S. Liabilities	4.2	11.1	16.0	61.5
British Liabilities	10.1	6.3	8.9	8.6[a]
Other Reserves	—	3.6	6.7	16.3
Special Drawing Rights	—	—	—	9.4
Reserve Positions in the Monetary Fund	—	3.6	6.7	6.9
Total Reserves	47.6	60.2	78.2	158.7
World exports during the year	34.2	113.4	244.5	368.0

Per cent of Total Monetary Reserves				
Total Reserves	100.0	100.0	100.0	100.0
Total Gold Reserves	70.0	63.1	50.0	24.8
U.S. Reserves	42.2	29.6	15.2	6.7
Foreign Exchange	30.0	30.9	41.4	64.9
U.S. Liabilities	8.8	18.4	20.4	39.2
British Liabilities	21.2	10.5	11.4	5.5[a]
Other Reserves	—	6.0	8.6	10.4
Special Drawing Rights	—	—	—	6.0
Reserve Positions in the Monetary Fund	—	6.0	8.6	4.4

[a] *As of November 1972.*
Source: IMF, International Financial Statistics, *May 1973 and earlier issues.*

continuing questions about the sustainability of the monetary gold price and the usefulness of gold as a basic measure of value.

Reliance on dollars as a source of international reserve creation suffers from the drawback that, in general, dollars can be added to international reserves only as a result of U.S. payments deficits. The use of U.S. deficits for this purpose worked well in the early postwar years when the world was short of dollars. Today it clearly is no longer satisfactory because many foreign monetary authorities have more dollars in their portfolios than they wish to hold. Indeed, reliance on dollars for reserve creation involves an inherent paradox. Although under this procedure new reserves can for the most part be generated only through U.S. payments deficits, continued deficits tend to undermine confidence in the dollar as such and therefore its usability as a reserve currency. Furthermore, as the experience of the past several years has demonstrated, a link between U.S. deficits and reserve creation can lead to tremendously wide and unplanned variations in the supply of new reserves.

If the international monetary system is to function properly, future reserve creation must be based on conscious management of international reserves tailored to the world's needs for liquidity and based on multilateral agreement. SDRs constitute the only reserve asset that is subject to such management and does not give rise to the confidence problems associated with gold or dollars. **We endorse the view that SDRs should be given increasing importance in the overall international monetary system, with the aim of eventually making them the principal international reserve asset; that they should be the system's formal numeraire, or "unit of account," against which changes in exchange rates or parities are measured; and that they should be freed of many of the operational limitations to which they are now subject. We also urge that gold be assigned a sharply diminishing role in the international monetary system and that its monetary role should eventually be abolished entirely.**

Reducing the Reserve Currency Role of the Dollar

If SDRs are to be given increasing importance as international reserve assets, it also follows that the relative importance of the dollar as a reserve currency must be reduced. Major questions remain, however, concerning how much of a reduction in the reserve currency role of the dollar is feasible and desirable. To what extent, in particular, should future reserve creation in the form of dollars be prevented by a requirement that the United States settle its deficits through reductions in its international reserve assets—a step that would imply the restoration of some form of dollar convertibility? And to what extent should dollars currently included in foreign official reserves be converted into other types of reserve assets?

The basic case for a reduction in the reserve currency role of the dollar (a role that in the earlier post-World War II period was in fact actively urged on the United States by other countries) rests on the belief that this role involves excessive asymmetries in the international monetary system. In the view of many foreign countries, particularly the Europeans, the asymmetry is primarily manifested in the fact that in recent years only the United States among the major nations (like the United Kingdom earlier) has been able to settle its deficits by increasing its liabilities (i.e., by having other countries hold growing amounts of its own currency). By contrast, countries whose currencies are not accepted as international reserves to the same degree as dollars generally must pay for deficits by giving up official reserve assets. It is argued that this procedure has given the United States an unfair advantage by enabling it to draw too readily on the resources of other countries. In this view, a reduction or elimination of the reserve currency role of the dollar and the restoration of dollar convertibility are required primarily to subject the United States to the same type of discipline over its economic policies that has long been imposed on other nations by the need to settle deficits in reserve assets.

From the U.S. viewpoint, on the other hand, the more serious asymmetry of the system lies elsewhere. It has been connected with the fact that the reserve currency role of the dollar—and its related use as the unit of account of the system—have tended to deprive the United States of adequate ability to devalue its currency in order to reduce its balance-of-payments deficits. This country has essentially lacked the power to devalue because to do so would impose heavy losses on the dollar holdings of other countries. At the same time, surplus countries have tended to be exceedingly slow in taking active steps to adjust their exchange rates or to take other measures to reduce their surpluses. These could have included, for example, further trade liberalization or a lifting of restrictions that inhibit or prevent investments by their nationals abroad. It is this set of circumstances, rather than a desire to exploit a special advantage, that accounts in considerable measure for the persistence of excessive U.S. deficits.

These considerations explain why the major industrial countries have a mutual interest in seeking a reduction in the reserve currency role of the dollar in its several dimensions and, by implication, in the restoration of some degree of dollar convertibility.* However, there is no quick or easy means of achieving such an outcome or of making the international monetary system fully symmetrical. The principal reason is that the dollar serves not only as a reserve currency but also as (1) the principal currency that central banks use for intervention in exchange markets and (2) the most important private transactions currency. Together with the basic economic strength of the United States, these factors create an inherent element of asymmetry in the international monetary system that cannot and should not be expected to be eliminated soon and that may persist for a long time.

The fact is that use of the dollar as the principal intervention and transactions currency has been a major source of convenience and economy for foreign monetary authorities as well as for business firms and financial institutions. In many cases, inclusion of dollars in monetary reserves has largely been a by-product of the use of dollars for other purposes. Recently, central banks have started to make increased use of other major currencies for intervention purposes, notably within the Common Market. But for the most part, the dollar has retained the key role in market intervention. As long as there is no clear, near-term alternative to reliance on the dollar as the major intervention and transactions currency, overly stringent limitations on its role as a source of international reserves may be neither feasible nor desirable.

Conditions for Dollar Convertibility

The practical difficulties that would confront any attempt to impose such limitations can be seen most clearly when consideration is given to the problems that would result from an early resumption of a

---

*See Memorandum by MR. JOHN B. CAVE, page 87.

high degree of dollar convertibility—a step urged by various European countries.[1]

First, the accumulated "overhang" of dollars in foreign official reserves is now about five times as large as the total of U.S. reserve assets of about $13 billion. This factor alone creates a risk that the potential claims for dollar conversions might be far larger than those arising in connection with the settlement of current U.S. payments deficits.

Second, even if adequate means were found to cope with the *existing* overhang of official foreign dollar holdings, there would be no assurance that total U.S. reserves would be large enough to cope adequately with all future conversion demands. One reason is that as long as the dollar remains the main currency that central banks use for intervention in foreign exchange markets, the settlement of payments imbalances among third countries can give rise to demands for conversions into U.S. reserve assets even at a time when the United States is running a payments surplus. Such demands might in particular be triggered by large-scale movements out of private foreign dollar balances that are not directly connected with the current U.S. payments situation. Moreover, the total of existing U.S. reserves is relatively small even in terms of any current deficits the United States might run. In relation to imports, for example, these reserves are smaller than those of most other countries. Furthermore, efforts to build up U.S. reserves through the accumulation of U.S. payments surpluses will be frustrated as long as foreign monetary authorities draw down dollar reserves in meeting their deficits.

Third, unless additional steps are taken to assure that the balance-of-payments adjustment process will in fact work more smoothly and equitably than in the past, return to convertibility of the dollar could well be unwise. It would not necessarily provide sufficient symmetry in international monetary relations to permit the strengthening of the U.S. payments position that is necessary to make convertibility viable over the long run. As long as the dollar continues to serve as the key intervention currency, the United States will have less power to affect its market ex-

---

1/It should be understood that the type of convertibility these countries seek to restore is *asset* convertibility, that is, convertibility of dollars held by foreign monetary authorities into official U.S. reserve assets. In private markets, the dollar for the most part has never ceased to be freely convertible into other currencies. This is the case principally because the U.S. government does not impose exchange controls that would prevent its citizens from exchanging U.S. dollars for other currencies at some price.

change rates than other countries. Moreover, the "discipline" that convertibility would exert on the United States could be one-sided and excessive. As already noted, drains on U.S. reserves could stem from influences that have no direct connection with the U.S. balance-of-payments performance. Moreover, convertibility obligations place pressures only on deficit countries; they do not exert any comparable discipline on nations that run excessive payments surpluses.

These considerations lead us to the following conclusions and recommendations:

1. **We believe that the United States should cooperate in international efforts to develop acceptable procedures for the eventual restoration of some form of dollar convertibility into reserve assets.** A move in this direction would be in the interest of all countries. It would help the United States to gain greater powers of initiative in changing its exchange rate. Moreover, indefinite continuation of complete inconvertibility of the dollar for official purposes is not likely to be acceptable to many other countries. Thus it runs the risk of leading to undesirable capital restrictions by these countries as well as to an increasing reliance on restrictive currency and trading blocs.

2. **At the same time, however, we strongly recommend against any U.S. agreement to a new convertibility obligation until arrangements have been worked out that will leave no doubt that this obligation can in fact be sustained.** An attempt to restore convertibility on unrealistic terms would be self-defeating. It would either require a renewed suspension of convertibility within a short time or place pressure on the United States to reintroduce capital controls and other direct measures to restrict its foreign transactions.

3. **We further recommend that the United States insist that a series of key conditions be met before restoration of some form of convertibility of the dollar into other official reserve assets can be considered. These conditions should be precisely articulated and must include (a) adequate provisions for improvement of the international adjustment mechanism; (b) satisfactory means of handling the overhang of outstanding official dollar holdings; (c) new procedures for coping with massive movements of funds; and (d) provisions for adequate international reserve allocation to the United States as well as to other countries.**

We have already discussed the requirements for an improved international adjustment process. We now turn to problems of the official dollar overhang and of possible means through which the United States could obtain adequate resources (in the form of either reserves or contingent credit facilities) to cope with massive fluctuations in private dollar holdings.

Coping with the Dollar Overhang in Both Official and Private Hands

Broadly speaking, the term "dollar overhang" refers to the accumulated total of dollars in foreign hands that foreign monetary authorities could use to convert into U.S. reserve assets once dollar convertibility is restored. Most commonly, the overhang is discussed in relation to part of the dollars now held by foreign monetary authorities. By the spring of 1973, the total of such official holdings had probably reached close to $70 billion. Others would add to this total all or part of foreign private dollar balances, including some $18 billion held in American banks plus at least a portion of an estimated $80 billion or more in the Eurodollar market.[2]

None of these numbers, however, gives a reliable indication of the total of potential claims on U.S. reserves. Many of the dollars in foreign official or private hands are held willingly, either as working balances or for precautionary and investment purposes. Thus, they do not necessarily constitute a true part of the overhang. Clearly, the extent to which foreigners will continue to hold dollars voluntarily depends to a major degree on their basic confidence in the dollar as an international currency. If the United States follows sound economic policies and shows increasing success in improving its payments position, the willingness of foreigners to hold dollars is likely to be increased. This could significantly reduce the size of the so-called overhang. Moreover, the size of the overhang would tend to be further diminished if other countries showed a greater willingness to remove existing restrictions on investments by their citizens abroad.

2/Eurodollars can in part be created independently of U.S. balance-of-payments developments and can at least indirectly lead to conversion demands by official monetary authorities.

With inappropriate U.S. policies and a poorly working adjustment process, on the other hand, the volume of foreign dollar holdings that might give rise to conversions would greatly increase. Indeed, with severe weakening of confidence, the problem of the overhang would no longer be confined to dollars in foreign hands. A far greater potential threat to dollar convertibility could stem from outflows of funds from the United States and their transformation into foreign official claims after they have been converted into other currencies or gold. In early 1973, the potential "overhang" of money and "near-money" located *within* the United States totaled almost $550 billion; and this is only a partial measure of the assets that U.S. residents could in principle seek to convert into foreign holdings. It is clear, therefore, that the most important means of reducing the potential threat of a dollar overhang is the pursuit of sound U.S. domestic economic policies. Such policies are essential to success in bringing the U.S. payments position into better balance.

Handling the Official Overhang. Even with the appropriate U.S. policies, however, eventual restoration of some form of asset convertibility of the dollar will clearly require steps to guard against excessive conversions of outstanding dollar balances that are unrelated to the settlement of U.S. deficits. Suggestions for dealing with this problem have included (1) some form of bilateral funding of short-term dollar holdings by foreign central banks into longer-term obligations not usable to finance balance-of-payments deficits and (2) an exchange of the dollars into a special issue of SDRs or some other international obligation through a new facility in the IMF.

Although we shall not attempt to offer a specific plan for coping with these problems, it is our view that any solution that is finally worked out should conform to the following broad principles:

1. **Arrangements for consolidating the overhang or restoring convertibility should in general not restrict countries from holding dollars in their official reserves as working balances and for related purposes if they so wish.** However, special procedures may have to be developed to assure that existing or future dollar holdings by foreign monetary authorities do not prevent the United States from accumulating reserve assets once its payments position moves into surplus.

2. **Since progress toward reducing the overhang and restoring some element of official dollar convertibility is in the interest of all coun-**

tries, any method that might be used for consolidating the overhang should involve an equitable international sharing of the burden with respect to such matters as interest-rate and maintenance-of-value provisions. The consolidation arrangements should not be based on a presumption that past accumulations of dollars in foreign hands are attributable solely to actions by the United States. It is true that unsound domestic economic policies were an important contributor to the large U.S. payments deficits. But it is also true that a significant part of the outflows was related to U.S. military and aid commitments abroad and that U.S. deficits would have been substantially smaller if other countries had helped to prevent an excessive accumulation of payments surpluses. This could have been done if these countries had taken more timely measures to readjust their exchange rates, opened their markets more freely to imports from the United States and elsewhere, and removed restrictions on capital investments by their citizens abroad. Moreover, an important share of the outflow consisted of funds that the United States provided as a world banker rather than as a trader. These funds were willingly accepted—and even sought—by other countries as a means of facilitating financial transactions. Indeed, the Bretton Woods system provided no other source of growth of world reserves. No useful purpose can be served by fruitless arguments over the precise causes that gave rise to the large dollar holdings in foreign hands.

3. **Any agreement on consolidation or restoration of convertibility must include adequate arrangements for permitting the United States to earn the extra current account surpluses and to receive the added investment inflows that are required to make the necessary transfers possible.** Even without a formal consolidation procedure, other countries can, of course, at any time obtain additional real resources from the United States for their accumulated dollars by allowing their citizens to purchase more American goods and services and to invest their capital here. A special consolidation arrangement might be designed to speed up this process, although care would have to be taken that the consolidation occurs over a sufficiently extended period to avoid undue strains on international payments relationships. Perhaps a procedure might also be devised under which consolidation of at least part of the overhang would be associated with an increase in overall development assistance by all major countries.

Dealing with Massive Movements of Funds. The consolidation of existing official foreign dollar balances would deal with only one of the potential threats to dollar convertibility. An even more serious threat stems from the possibility of massive conversion into official balances of dollars that remain in private hands. Here, too, sound U.S. economic policies and better procedures for payments adjustment are of basic importance in reducing the magnitude of the threat. In addition, greater exchange rate flexibility, including wider margins around parities or central rates, can itself lessen the scope for volatile capital movements. But even with such reforms, the "overhang" of private dollars, domestic as well as foreign, will remain a significant potential threat to the stability of the monetary system.

We believe that the most promising approach for dealing with the problem would be the creation of an international financing capability sufficiently powerful to (1) inhibit the emergence of massive speculative pressures on the system and (2) offset exceptionally large and sudden capital flows when this seems necessary to preserve the viability of the system and avoid widespread resort to capital controls.

There are a number of approaches that can be used in this context. At present the principal means of coping with highly destabilizing capital movements is the use of so-called swap facilities permitting the mutual extension of short-term credit by central banks to each other. However, the size and character of the existing swap facilities are far from adequate to cope convincingly with the potential problems that might arise if, at some future date, a form of official dollar convertibility were to be reestablished. **We therefore recommend the creation of a much more powerful special lending facility in the IMF that would be capable of coping with massive movements of funds that might threaten to undermine a new U.S. convertibility obligation or the convertibility obligation of any other country. To assure that the facility would be used only in appropriate situations, its activation should require approval by the Fund's Managing Director.**[3] Special guidelines governing his decisions on activation would have to be developed to make certain that the facility would be used only to counter severe threats to convertibility; it should not serve as an instrument for preventing adequate exchange rate flexibility.

3/A similar proposal has recently been advanced by Professor Richard N. Cooper of Yale University. Under Professor Cooper's proposal, however, use of the facility would not require such prior approval.

Once the Managing Director of the IMF decided that activation of the facility was warranted there would, by international agreement, be no limit to the amount of short-term credit that could in such situations be extended to cover exceptionally large and sudden conversions of one currency into another. If the flow of funds were to be reversed within a relatively short period, as would usually be expected, the special credit would be promptly repaid. If the movements failed to reverse themselves within a specified time, the balances might be funded into long-term repayable obligations. Or if it turned out that part of or all the large currency flow had been due to a worsening of a country's basic balance-of-payments position, the country in question might have to repay the IMF over an intermediate-term period. If necessary, this could be done by drawing on the Fund's normal lending facilities. In either case, the new rules for the adjustment process would have to assure that the country incurring the obligation could run the payments surpluses necessary to repay its debt.

Chapter Five

Improving
International Institutions and Procedures

As we indicated at the beginning of this statement, a central feature of any basic improvement in the functioning of the world monetary system must be a major strengthening of international monetary institutions, rules, and procedures.

At present, authority in international monetary matters is divided among a series of organizations. The most important of these include the International Monetary Fund, the Committee of 20, the Group of Ten, Working Party III of OECD, and the Basle group of central banks. Various related functions are carried out by such organizations as GATT and by different OECD committees concerned with capital movements. None of these bodies possesses the degree of authority and ability to compel compliance with internationally agreed-upon rules that are needed for a really satisfactory functioning of the world monetary system.

Broadening the Powers of the International Monetary Fund

We believe that the principal powers of international monetary management under the proposed new arrangements should be lodged in the International Monetary Fund. This will call for basic changes in the

Fund's articles and administrative organization. Among the functions of a strengthened IMF should be the following:

First, the Fund should become the focal point for more effective multilateral consultations on the full range of policies needed to achieve better balance-of-payments adjustment. Such consultations should be designed to force member countries to face up to the underlying factors that impede satisfactory adjustment. They should also seek to develop a clearer understanding of areas where longer-run mutuality of interests exists; the common need of the developed countries to cope with the balance-of-payments implications of future energy and materials requirements is an important example. The consultations would have to concentrate intensively on the interrelationship and mutual consistency of member countries' balance-of-payments objectives. These should include their aims with respect to balance-of-payments structure, such as the relationship between current account and capital account transactions.

Second, the IMF should have the central role in the development, application, and interpretation of rules governing the management of both par (or central) value and floating exchange rate systems. This function should include the construction of various presumptive indicators for adjustment and the triggering of procedures and actions called for by these indicators. It should also involve the development of better and more consistent criteria regarding the permissible use of different adjustment policy instruments. This would require a more intensive effort than has been made to date in order to arrive at an integrated set of understandings regarding the appropriate use in different situations of demand-management policy, exchange rate adjustment, and measures directly affecting trade and capital movements.

Third, the IMF should have ample powers to monitor the extent of compliance with the newly developed rules and to authorize the eventual application of sanctions against noncompliers under internationally established procedures. Unlike existing IMF compliance provisions (which have mainly affected deficit countries through the power to withhold financing), such sanctions should apply equally to surplus and deficit countries. Their application should be carefully graduated in terms of forcefulness. Initial stress would be placed on exhortation and then on new types of financial penalties, such as the withholdings of new

SDR allocations. Only in extreme situations should there be authorization of measures involving exchange restrictions or discriminatory trade restraints such as import surcharges. It is hoped, of course, that actual resort to sanctions would not be necessary once the authority to apply them has been clearly established.

Fourth, the IMF (or agencies operating under its direction) should be given certain added operational functions that can best be carried out by a central international organization, along lines indicated earlier. In particular, these should include the power to activate a special lending facility that could cope decisively with massive flows of funds that threaten to disrupt the stability of the monetary system. Eventually, the Fund might also be given responsibility for certain types of intervention in floating exchange markets, such as intervention for smoothing purposes to be carried out in accordance with internationally agreed-upon standards.

The new powers of the IMF envisaged here would call for a significantly greater willingness of member governments to submit to common rules and cooperative procedures. Moreover, if the new arrangements are to be effective, the IMF will ultimately have to gain some elements of independence in interpreting and applying the rules and to play a more active role in recommending needed changes in adjustment policies. Such increased powers imply that the Fund's member countries would have to yield some added elements of national sovereignty to this international institution.

Clearly, any added authority for the Fund cannot be based on legal powers alone. The system can work only if there is a political will to make it work. It presupposes that the major nations will be in fundamental political agreement to surrender some elements of their independence to an international body of which they are a part. The successes of the Bretton Woods system, it should be noted, were based on such an underlying willingness to cooperate.

It will certainly not be easy to arrive at the needed agreement. We believe, however, that a satisfactory agreement can be reached once the top political officials as well as the technical experts understand clearly that, on balance, the proposed strengthening of the IMF will be to the mutual benefit of all countries. Of course, steps to increase its power should not be taken lightly or without firm commitment that member countries will in fact be willing to abide by the new arrangements. The United States, in particular, should insist that any formal enlargement of the powers of the Fund constitute an integral part of a satisfactory overall agreement for international monetary reform. Above all, there must be assurance that the agreement will place equal responsibilities for payments adjustment on surplus and deficit countries and will provide for major improvements in adjustment procedures.

If the added functions and powers of the Fund are to be made effective, the Fund itself must be reorganized and strengthened. We believe that the following changes would be particularly desirable:

1. **The level of country representation in the IMF's major decision-making body must be high enough to allow this body to serve without question as the principal continuing focal point for international monetary coordination and management.** The Fund's Executive Board does not meet this requirement at present because the Executive Directors are normally outranked within their own governments by their country's representatives in such other international bodies as Working Party III of OECD. An appropriate change would be to retain much of the structure of the present Executive Board in terms of size and distribution of country representation but to provide that member countries substitute top-level officials as their representatives on the Board whenever this seems appropriate. The result would be that the more important deliberations and decisions in the Fund would be carried out by high-level officials who would travel to the Fund's headquarters from national capitals at frequent intervals. It is noteworthy that a comparable procedure has recently been successfully employed to upgrade the level of representation on the Executive Committee of the OECD.

2. **The internal structure and working procedures of the IMF should be more clearly directed at emphasizing the mutual responsibilities of surplus and deficit countries in the adjustment process.** At present, IMF procedures are predominantly geared to individual country examinations, on the model of a bank's relationships with loan applicants. This is far less satisfactory for dealing with the interrelated problems facing major surplus and deficit countries than the mutual confrontation procedures employed in OECD. Although individual country examinations should be retained, the Fund's deliberative procedures and research activities need to be reorganized to facilitate intensive examinations of

the mutual consistency of the payments aims, structures, and policies of the member countries.

3. **To allow the IMF to cope more effectively with special functional issues that impinge on the international monetary system—such as the role of the Eurodollar market, the world energy problem, and trade policies—the upgraded Fund Board should make use of special committees or working groups that can focus more intensively on such issues than is possible for the Board as a whole.** The recommendations of such committees would, of course, remain subject to final approval of the full Fund Board.

4. **Additional procedures should be developed to allow the IMF to focus more directly on the interrelationship of international monetary problems with trade, investment, tax, and related considerations. There is also a need for better coordination of the Fund's activities with those of other organizations that deal with these matters.**

Other Institutional Improvements

The experience of recent years has made it increasingly clear that international monetary problems must inevitably be considered in conjunction with a wide range of other economic issues. The close relationship between monetary and trade matters, for example, was highlighted by the President's temporary use of an import surcharge as a bargaining device to secure a better overall agreement on payments adjustment. The future role of the European Community's Common Agricultural Policy was a key element in the subsequent negotiations for a basic realignment of exchange rates. Moreover, national policies with respect to the treatment of foreign investment, taxation, nontariff barriers, antitrust laws, environmental standards, and many other economic issues pose continuous questions for international monetary management.

Although a strengthened IMF should be a focal point for considering the interrelationship of these policies and their relevance to the adjustment process, there will be continuing need for various specialized organizations that can concentrate on particular types of policies. The roles of GATT in the field of trade and of the OECD in such areas as foreign aid and capital movements are clear examples. However, additional initiatives are required to (1) develop needed new forms of international cooperation and standards of behavior, notably in such fields as direct investment and energy; (2) assure that the rules for international economic behavior developed by different institutions are consistent with one another, with a clear assignment of particular functions to each; and (3) provide for more adequate liaison among the institutions.

One key requirement is to develop a closer and more clearly defined relationship between the IMF and the GATT. In particular, there is a need to eliminate inconsistencies between existing GATT rules and the codes of behavior that can be expected to emerge under a reformed international monetary system. At present, for example, GATT rules permit the use of import quotas to help overcome temporary balance-of-payments difficulties but rule out uniform import surcharges and export subsidies for this purpose. This is contrary to the emerging consensus among international monetary officials that if trade restrictions are to be used for balance-of-payments purposes at all, they should preferably consist of measures that work through the price mechanism rather than quantitative restrictions. A major need also exists to develop acceptable international standards and surveillance procedures with respect to temporary "safeguards" against very sudden and disruptive import increases.

In the area of foreign investment, we reiterate the recommendation in our November 1971 statement, *The United States and the European Community: Policies for a Changing World Economy,*[1] that "a major multilateral effort be made to deal with the important issues involving national policies toward foreign investment. The objective should be to reach agreement among the industrialized countries on a consistent set of rules governing the treatment of foreign investment, including the extraterritorial application of national policies and the use of policies which discriminate against foreign-based enterprises."

We also believe that new guidelines for international rationalization of agriculture must be a major subject for multilateral negotiation. If import restrictions and export subsidies are to be moderated in agricultural trade, limits will have to be placed on domestic price supports in

---

1/ *The United States and the European Community: Policies for a Changing World Economy,* A Statement on National Policy by the Research and Policy Committee, Committee for Economic Development (New York: November 1971).

the major producing and trading countries.[2] Moreover, a concerted international effort is required to cope with the mounting world energy problems.

In the recent past, systematic efforts have begun within the OECD to develop an agenda for actions needed to achieve a better coordination of activities in all these areas and to bring about a more rational distribution of functions among international economic institutions. It is to be hoped that these efforts will serve as the basis for major progress toward the harmonization of international economic policies.

2/See *An Adaptive Program for Agriculture,* A Statement on National Policy by the Research and Policy Committee, Committee for Economic Development (New York: July 1962).

Chapter Six

International Monetary
Reform and Development Assistance

An issue that has given rise to considerable controversy in the current monetary negotiations involves the form and extent of a possible "link" between international monetary reform and an enlarged and steadier flow of development assistance to the less developed countries (LDCs). This matter has a special significance for the outcome of the negotiations because many of these countries apparently feel that the overall reform package might not prove acceptable to them unless it contains an explicit provision for such a link.

In reviewing this issue, it is important to note that a successful reform of the international monetary system would by itself be of major benefit to the less developed countries, whether or not a formal provision for a "link" is included in any eventual international accord. To be sure, many of these countries are at present somewhat fearful that a reformed system involving increased exchange rate flexibility for the developed nations might expose their own international transactions to excessive risks. It seems clear, however, that on balance the approach toward strengthening the world monetary system outlined in this policy statement will be to the advantage of all countries. By reducing the size of payments imbalances and preventing the recurrence of monetary crises, it should enable the more advanced nations to follow more stable domestic economic policies and avoid frequent lapses into recession. This should assure expanded and steadier demands for the products of the less developed countries. In addition, these countries will be greatly aided as improvements in the adjustment process permit the removal of onerous restrictions on trade, aid, and capital movements that many of the industrial countries now impose for balance-of-payments reasons.

The success of the international monetary reform, in turn, will depend partly on the viability of the emerging economic and payments relationships between the developed and the less developed nations. Even with a significantly increased demand for the products of the less developed countries, a properly functioning world economy and payments system is likely to call for an increased and more regular flow of private and public capital resources to the poorer countries.

It is the desire to make more adequate flows of capital resources to the less developed nations an automatic and regular feature of the international economic system that has given the major impetus to the more controversial proposals for a link between international monetary reform and development aid. Under these proposals, the creation and use of new international liquidity in the form of SDRs would be directly and formally linked to the provision of increased capital assistance to the less developed countries. This might, for example, mean that a specified percentage of each new SDR issue would be directly allocated to an international development agency, such as the International Development Association (IDA). Or it might involve agreement by the more advanced countries to transfer to IDA a predetermined proportion of the SDRs they receive with each new SDR issue.

We believe that if the proposed international monetary reforms are to be successful over the longer term, they should be paralleled by active efforts on the part of the world's more affluent nations to increase the quantity and quality of assistance to the less developed countries. We also feel that the less developed countries should receive an equitable share of initial SDR allocations. There is nothing sacrosanct about the existing formula for distributing SDRs.

Appropriate changes in the formula for allocating SDRs should be considered in instances where it may not adequately reflect the liquidity needs of individual countries; this may well call for an increase in SDR

allocations to less developed nations. However, we recommend against the establishment of an automatic link between the creation of SDRs and development assistance. The amount of SDRs issued should not be based on criteria other than liquidity needs and the proper functioning of the international monetary system. In our view, an automatic link would tend to endanger the acceptability and workability of SDRs and of the proposed international monetary reform as a whole, particularly in their early stages.* On balance, it would be against the interests of the developing as well as the developed countries.

Our position is based on three principal considerations:

First, the attempt to use SDRs to achieve two quite distinct objectives at the same time is likely to mean that neither objective will be properly served. The essence of the SDR system is to provide countries with reserves that are appropriate to their liquidity, or cash balance, needs. It should satisfy their demand for money to hold rather than for money to spend. The aim of a system of development assistance, on the other hand, is the transfer of real resources to the less developed countries. This *requires* that the new SDRs be spent. A rigid link cannot serve these two aims simultaneously.

Adoption of proposals for an automatic link would involve a danger that decisions about SDR creation and use will be unduly affected by considerations that are unrelated to liquidity needs. It might also lead to an inequitable and haphazard distribution of the aid burden among donor countries. By contrast, when aid is allocated without reference to SDRs, each donor country's share of the burden can be based on an appropriate yardstick of capacity to pay, such as total or per capita GNP.

Second, a related drawback of the link is its potential for adding to inflation. When it is known in advance that the amount of extra development assistance that will become available is a fixed percentage of each new SDR allocation, pressures are bound to arise to make such allocations as large as possible. This will occur whether or not a larger allocation is justified in terms of international liquidity needs. Moreover, a link arrangement may also prove somewhat more inflationary than the present system as far as the usage of SDRs is concerned. A portion of the newly issued SDRs would be available for development assistance, whether or

---

*See Memoranda by MR. LINCOLN GORDON and MR. DAVIDSON SOMMERS, pages 85 and 86.

not the country receiving them is in balance-of-payments deficit. Without a link, only countries in deficit would normally use SDRs for settlement.

Third, use of SDRs for development purposes would in effect be a form of "backdoor" financing of foreign aid. Adoption of the link would thus run directly counter to CED's long-standing position in support of stricter budgetary control and a more forthright facing up to budget priorities. We believe that the need to stand by and reemphasize this position is currently more urgent than ever. Greater fiscal responsibility is of central importance for the strengthening of confidence in the dollar that is essential for the success of international monetary reform.

The basic developmental goals that proponents of the "link" seek to achieve, including enlarged and more regular development assistance through multilateral channels, can be just as effectively attained through such existing procedures as the provision of congressionally voted funds to the IDA—provided the Congress is willing to grant such aid. If this underlying willingness is not present, it is highly doubtful that Congress would accept an SDR link as a device to increase the total amount of U.S. development assistance. Even if such a procedure were initially adopted, it could soon prove counterproductive. To the extent it came to be resented as a device to circumvent the regular congressional budgetary process, it might well lead to cuts in other forms of foreign assistance that would more than offset the additional aid generated through the link arrangement.

Although we reject a *mechanical* linkage between SDR creation and development aid, we believe that positive steps are required to assure more adequate long-term capital flows to the less developed nations. Moreover, concern with such flows should become an integral part of improved international adjustment procedures. **We recommend that any agreement on international monetary reform be paralleled by a strengthening of multilateral commitments for a more adequate provision of development assistance to the less developed countries, with aid burdens based on appropriate indicators of national economic strength. We further recommend that in-depth consideration of the balance-of-payments relationships between the developed and less developed nations and their implications for the needed flow and form of development assistance become a required feature of the improved IMF procedures with respect to international monetary adjustment.**

It is in the context of such procedures that constructive new initiatives can best be developed to harmonize the needs for an improved process of payments adjustment and for more adequate resource transfers to "third world" countries. As indicated in Chapter Four, for example, arrangements might be worked out through which the real resources made available by the United States in connection with any funding of the dollar "overhang" would in effect be channeled largely to the less developed nations.

The international monetary consultations should also face up to the likelihood that, given present trends, by 1980 the current account surpluses of the oil-producing countries vis-à-vis the industrial nations may well be equal in size to the current account surpluses of the industrial nations in relation to the non-oil-producing LDCs. This suggests the need to devise orderly and cooperative arrangements under which a significant part of the large current account surpluses that the oil-producing countries may generate will in effect be utilized to channel resources to the world's poorer nations. At the same time, pressure on industrial countries to run large current account surpluses would tend to be reduced.

In these areas as in other aspects of strengthening the international monetary and economic systems, purely mechanical approaches are not likely to be adequate to cope with the complex problems that are bound to emerge in the decades ahead. Effective solutions will require major improvements in the processes of international consultation and cooperation and a strong political will to make these improvements possible.

Memoranda
of Comment, Reservation,
or Dissent

Page 11—By THEODORE O. YNTEMA, with which JOHN D. HARPER has asked to be associated:

I applaud this paper for its central theme, but I wish it were less digressive, less regressive, and much shorter. It seems to me there are three points to be made. International financial arrangements and agreements should:

1. Recognize the primary role of exchange rates in preventing and correcting fundamental imbalances in international payments.

2. Prohibit or limit the use of tariffs, quotas, etc. as substitutes for exchange rate adjustment.

3. Limit the extent of interference by governments in exchange rate markets. We should welcome the role of speculators in keeping us honest and anticipating troubles before they overwhelm us. Even the underdeveloped countries would fare better if they let their exchange rates conform more closely to realistic market levels.

Pages 21 and 49—By JOHN D. HARPER:

I can generally agree with this statement but I do not at all agree that incomes policies or controls are valuable in restraining inflation. I think it is very poor judgment for CED to imply that incomes policies can restrain inflation when such control policies have proven to be unworkable all over the world.

Page 23—By FRANKLIN A. LINDSAY, with which GABRIEL HAUGE has asked to be associated:

In the future the dangers of over reaction to balance-of-payments disequilibria may be as great as the dangers of excessive delay in adjusting exchange rates. As pointed out later in the report, the mechanisms by which a change in exchange rates works its way through the international trade and payments system are complex, and are likely to take a long time before a new equilibrium is fully achieved. The short term effects of a devaluation are likely to work in reverse to the long term expected results, because imports in the pipeline cost the devaluing country more and receipts from exports are less. In the midterm, exports of the devaluing country must increase by more than the devaluation before the desired impact begins to be felt. This means, for example, that sales organizations must be redirected to take advantage of their new competitive price advantages and companies must develop and produce new or modified products for foreign sale. This takes time. Only after decisions on the location of new plants to serve international markets begin to be made in light of changed cost structures, and these new plants are built and in production, will the full impact of the changes in exchange rates be felt. Thus if the expected change in balance-of-payments fails to appear after several months, or even after two or three years, the proposed indicators may signal further changes in rates which in the longer run will be seen to have been over-correction.

If the IMF assumes broadened monetary management responsibilities, it should establish objective measures of the lag time that must be expected in the balance-of-payments response to changes in exchange rates. Without this projection of the expected delay before the balance of payments responds there will be a major danger that governments will be pressured prematurely into further rate changes that later turn out to have gone too far.

Page 24—By GABRIEL HAUGE:

Both in this policy recommendation and in the body of the text, an evenhanded approach is taken on the issue of whether future international monetary arrangements should be based on a par value system or on a floating system. While I agree that an immediate choice in this matter is not urgent and that the period ahead may yield relevant experience, I would have preferred that the Statement take a clear position favoring a system of parities as the objective to be sought. While a par value system with greater flexibility and a floating system under agreed rules (which seems to me essential in the light of the capital controls now proliferating) may not be all that different in practice, I believe the former would be easier to define and administer. Its encouragement to the pursuit of sensible domestic policies by the principal nations would also be greater in my opinion.

Page 25—By ROBERT O. ANDERSON, with which JOHN D. HARPER and FRANKLIN A. LINDSAY have asked to be associated:

President Nixon's statement of June 13, 1973, recommending a two-tiered price system and export controls on agricultural, wood products and petroleum indicates a continued preoccupation with domestic consumer price that is totally inconsistent with the realities of today's international monetary problems and world trade.

Devaluation of the dollar has placed a number of U.S. commodities in a very attractive position, yet when such badly needed export markets emerge we are apparently unwilling to permit these products to move freely in world commerce and at the world price level.

Our present controlled economic policies may be politically opportune but they constitute a continuing threat to a free and stable monetary system.

The U.S. must realize that a strong and stable currency requires sacrifices in the form of exports when imbalances occur. Until we are prepared to take such courageous action, the outlook for a stronger dollar appears remote.

Pages 31 and 80—By LINCOLN GORDON, with which DAVIDSON SOMMERS and ROBERT R. NATHAN have asked to be associated:

In this otherwise admirable policy statement, I continue to be troubled by the thrust of the argument against an automatic link between multilateral development assistance channeled through international financing institutions and the creation of SDRs to meet growing world needs for liquidity. Such a link *need not* "endanger the acceptability and workability" of the reformed monetary system. It could be made entirely compatible with the system. If it becomes a negotiating prerequisite to the support of the less developed countries for overall reform, the United States should not oppose it on principle.

The text fails to distinguish adequately between the overall volume of SDRs, which should be based exclusively on world liquidity needs, and the initial allocation of new SDRs to particular countries. There is a welcome reference to a distribution formula more favorable to developing countries than the present one. But the phrase "liquidity needs of individual countries" and the concern (page 80) that some countries might get SDRs even though not in balance-of-payments deficit imply that country allocations should somehow be related to persistent deficits.

In a theoretically perfect system, there would be neither persistent deficits nor persistent surpluses. Every country would be in equilibrium year in and year out as a result of smoothly working adjustment mechanisms. Liquidity would then be needed only to finance seasonal or other very short-term fluctuations. Its country allocation would be based on the volume of each country's current transactions and the amplitude of its typical seasonal fluctuations.

In the real world, however well reformed, domestic considerations will inevitably create lags in adjustments and lead to surpluses or deficits more persistent than the theoretical ideal. The surplus countries will have no need for additional liquidity. The deficit countries will have such a need precisely because they have used up some of their reserve margins to acquire real resources.

Why not then require that a substantial portion of newly-created SDRs be earned? Their assignment to international financing institutions would require developing countries to earn them by making an effective case for allocations, while the industrialized countries would earn them through competitive sales of capital equipment to the original recipients. The overall volume would still be held to international liquidity needs, but the country allocations would help meet the declared objective (page 11) of "an international economic order that will benefit all countries."

Pages 31 and 80—By DAVIDSON SOMMERS:

Although I favor allocating SDR's to the developing countries in greater proportion than would be indicated by IMF quotas, I do not advocate an automatic link formula at the present stage. However I take this position as a matter of tactics rather than principle. I am not persuaded by the paper's arguments against an automatic link. I agree with Dr. Gordon's comments on these arguments.

Page 44—By HERMAN L. WEISS, with which JOHN D. HARPER has asked to be associated:

This recognition of the limited economic consequences of exchange rate changes deserves greater emphasis—especially in view of the ineffectiveness of the Smithsonian Agreement on the U.S. Balance of Payments.

It is well known that most European countries are committed to foster their own advanced-technology industries, e.g., computers, nuclear reactors, mass transportation equipment, telecommunications systems, electrical generating machinery. Since all these technologies require large-scale operations, most European Governments try to limit imports of these politically sensitive products. As a result, American exports lag behind their potential, although we frequently enjoy a comparative cost advantage. Further price reductions through additional dollar devaluations may, therefore, not improve U.S. exports to countries with the greatest ability to pay and with the largest demand for those products in which U.S. industry excels.

For years U.S. negotiators have discussed this problem within the OECD but with few tangible results. One can only hope that growing concern about the monetary disequilibrium will encourage our trading partners to adopt a more liberal attitude with respect to imports of high-technology products.

Page 63—By JOHN B. CAVE:

In Chapter 4 the subject of dollar convertibility is dealt with and while the statement supports convertibility it seems to me it takes a rather passive position towards the importance of convertibility. In my judgment an early move towards establishing dollar convertibility is highly important. Since the dollar will by necessity remain a major reserve currency for some time to come and since many of our friends abroad express great reluctance to hold any currency which is non-convertible, it seems to me that in order to restore confidence in the dollar and enhance the holding of dollars by foreign central banks and investors, the early restoration of its convertibility is a paramount consideration.

CED Board of Trustees

Honorary Trustees

Trustees on Leave for Government Service

CED Professional and Administrative Staff

PUBLICATION ORDER FORM

To order CED publications please indicate number in column entitled "# Copies Desired." Then mail this order form and check for total amount in envelope to Distribution Division, CED, 477 Madison Ave., New York 10022.

ORDER NUMBER STATEMENTS ON NATIONAL POLICY (paperbound) **# COPIES DESIRED**

51P . . STRENGTHENING THE WORLD MONETARY SYSTEM $1.50 _____
Recommends a program of basic reforms in the international monetary system, including the establishment of new rules to assure needed adjustments in currency exchange rates by both surplus and deficit countries.

50P . . FINANCING THE NATION'S HOUSING NEEDS $1.50 _____
Examines the financal obstacles that hinder fulfillment of the nation's housing requirements and sets forth recommendations to make the nation's housing markets more responsive to the needs of all sectors of society.

49P . . BUILDING A NATIONAL HEALTH-CARE SYSTEM $1.75 _____
Sets forth a plan for the organization, management, and financing of a national health care system which would improve the delivery of health care services while extending insurance coverage to all Americans.

48P . . A NEW TRADE POLICY TOWARD COMMUNIST COUNTRIES $1.50 _____
Recommends a continued easing of U.S. trade and credit restrictions against communist countries, bringing them in line with U.S. policies toward other industrialized nations.

47P . . HIGH EMPLOYMENT WITHOUT INFLATION: A POSITIVE PROGRAM FOR ECONOMIC STABILIZATION $1.50 _____
Recommends a continued governmnetal role in wage-price policies, calls for basic structural changes in the economy, and urges an incentive system of decontrol. Emphasizes that fiscal and monetary policies must remain the key element of the nation's economic efforts.

46P . . REDUCING CRIME AND ASSURING JUSTICE $1.50 _____
An integrated examination of needed reforms in the entire system of criminal justice, including courts, prosecution, police, and corrections.

45P . . MILITARY MANPOWER AND NATIONAL SECURITY $1.00 _____
Focuses on several critical issues relating to military manpower.

44P . . THE UNITED STATES AND THE EUROPEAN COMMUNITY $1.50 _____
Deals with the development of the Common Market into an enlarged European Economic Community and its potential effects on Western European trade, investment, and monetary relations with the U.S. and other free-world nations. Recommends immediate steps to halt deterioration in the world trading system.

43P . . IMPROVING FEDERAL PROGRAM PERFORMANCE $1.50 _____
Focuses attention on three major areas of concern about federal programs: (1) the choice of policy goals and program objectives, (2) the selection of programs that will achieve those objectives, and (3) the execution of the programs and the evaluation of their performance.

42P . . SOCIAL RESPONSIBILITIES OF BUSINESS CORPORATIONS $1.50 _____
Develops a rationale for corporate involvement in solving such pressing social problems as urban blight, poverty, and pollution. Examines the need for the corporation to make its social responsibilities an integral part of its business objectives. Points out at the same time the proper limitations on such activities.

41P . . EDUCATION FOR THE URBAN DISADVANTAGED: From Preschool to Employment $1.50 _____
A comprehensive review of the current state of education for disadvantaged minorities; sets forth philosophical and operational principles which are imperative if the mission of the urban schools is to be accomplished successfully.

40P . . FURTHER WEAPONS AGAINST INFLATION $1.50 _____
Examines the problem of reconciling high employment and price stability. Maintains that measures to supplement general fiscal and monetary policies will be needed—including the use of voluntary wage-price (or "incomes") policies, as well as measures to change the structural and institutional environment in which demand policy operates.

39P . . MAKING CONGRESS MORE EFFECTIVE $1.00 _____
Points out the structural and procedural handicaps limiting the ability of Congress to respond to the nation's needs. Proposes a far-reaching Congressional reform program.

38P . . DEVELOPMENT ASSISTANCE TO SOUTHEAST ASIA $1.50 _____
Deals with the importance of external resources—financial, managerial, and technological, including public and private—to the development of Southeast Asia.

37P . . TRAINING AND JOBS FOR THE URBAN POOR $1.25 _____
Explores ways of abating poverty that arises from low wages and chronic unemployment or underemployment. Evaluates current manpower training and employment efforts by government and business.

SEE OTHER SIDE→

ORDER NUMBER		# COPIES DESIRED

36P .. IMPROVING THE PUBLIC WELFARE SYSTEM — $1.50 _____
Analyzes the national problem of poverty and the role played by the present welfare system. The statement recommends major changes in both the rationale and the administration of the public assistance program, with a view to establishing need as the sole criterion for coverage.

35P .. RESHAPING GOVERNMENT IN METROPOLITAN AREAS — $1.00 _____
Recommends a two-level system of government for metropolitan areas: an area-wide level and a local level comprised of "community districts."

34P .. ASSISTING DEVELOPMENT IN LOW-INCOME COUNTRIES — $1.25 _____
Offers a sound rationale for public support of the U.S. economic assistance program and recommends a far-ranging set of priorities for U.S. Government policy.

33P .. NONTARIFF DISTORTIONS OF TRADE — $1.00 _____
Examines the complex problem of dealing with nontariff distortions of trade arising from governmental measures that create special barriers to imports and incentives to exports.

32P .. FISCAL AND MONETARY POLICIES FOR STEADY ECONOMIC GROWTH — $1.00 _____
Reexamines the role of fiscal and monetary policies in achieving the basic economic objectives of high employment, price stability, economic growth, and equilibrium in the nation's international payments.

31P .. FINANCING A BETTER ELECTION SYSTEM — $1.00 _____
Urges comprehensive modernization of election and campaign procedures at national, state, and local levels. Proposes ways to reduce costs and spread them more widely through tax credits.

30P .. INNOVATION IN EDUCATION — $1.00 _____
Examines the problems of the American schools, reviews educational goals and opportunities (including technological resources), and explores relative costs and benefits. Sets forth comprehensive recommendations for change.

28P .. MODERNIZING STATE GOVERNMENT — $1.00 _____
Recommends sweeping renovation of state governments and their constitutions. Proposes granting legislatures broad powers to deal with problems of a rapidly-changing era; strengthening executive capability through modern management methods; improving the administration of justice; and furthering intergovernmental relations.

27P .. TRADE POLICY TOWARD LOW-INCOME COUNTRIES — $1.50 _____

24P .. HOW LOW INCOME COUNTRIES CAN ADVANCE THEIR OWN GROWTH — $1.50 _____

23P .. MODERNIZING LOCAL GOVERNMENT — $1.00 _____

22P .. A BETTER BALANCE IN FEDERAL TAXES ON BUSINESS — 75¢ _____

21P .. BUDGETING FOR NATIONAL OBJECTIVES — $1.00 _____

15P .. EDUCATING TOMORROW'S MANAGERS — $1.00 _____

14P .. IMPROVING EXECUTIVE MANAGEMENT IN THE FEDERAL GOVERNMENT — $1.50 _____

9P .. ECONOMIC LITERACY FOR AMERICANS — 75¢ _____

1P .. ECONOMIC GROWTH IN THE UNITED STATES — $1.00 _____

Quantity discounts: 10-24 copies—10%, 25-49 copies—15%, 50-99 copies—20%, 100-249 copies—30%

NOTE TO EDUCATORS: Instructors in colleges and universities may obtain up to 5 free copies of those CED Statements on National Policy which they intend to use in courses they are teaching. **Please mention the course name when ordering.** For more than 5 copies, an educational discount of 20% will apply.

Course..

☐ I am enclosing $............................ for the copies ordered above.

☐ Please bill me. *(Payment must accompany orders under $10.00)*

DO YOU WANT ALL CED PUBLICATIONS WHEN ISSUED?

☐ I would like to obtain all CED publications as soon as they are issued. Please send me information about the CED Reader Forum subscription plan.

☐ Please send me newest list of publications.

Name..

Organization..

Address..

City.............................. State.............................. Zip..............................

☐ Businessman ☐ Educator ☐ Professional

TEAR OUT ON DOTTED LINE AND MAIL IN ENVELOPE TO CED

 **INTERNATIONAL LIBRARY**

Increasingly close relationships are being developed with independent, nonpolitical research organizations in other countries. These organizations are composed of businessmen and scholars, have objectives similar to those of CED, and pursue them by similarly objective methods. In several cases, agreements for reciprocal distribution of publications have developed out of this cooperation.

CEDA

Committee for Economic Development of Australia
343 Little Collins Street, Melbourne, Victoria

CEPES

Europäische Vereinigung für
Wirtschaftliche und Soziale Entwicklung
56 Friedrichstrasse, Dusseldorf, West Germany

PEP

Political and Economic Planning
12 Upper Belgrave Street,
London, SWIX 8BB, England

経済同友会

Keizai Doyukai
(Japan Committee for Economic Development)
Japan Industrial Club Bldg.
1 Marunouchi, Chiyoda-ku, Tokyo, Japan

CED

Council for Economic Development
Economic Development Foundation
P.O. Box 1896, Makati, Rizal, Philippines

CRC

Centre de Recherches et d'Etudes des Chefs d'Entreprise
31 Avenue Pierre 1er de Serbie, Paris (16eme), France

SNS

Studieförbundet Näringsliv och Samhälle
Sköldungagatan 2, 11427 Stockholm, Sweden

ESSCB

Ekonomik ve Sosyal Etüdler Konferans Heyeti
279/8 Cumhuriyet Cad. Adli Han
Harbiye, Istanbul, Turkey

COMMITTEE FOR
ECONOMIC DEVELOPMENT